D0226921

Sister Philothea

Sister Philothea

Relationships between Women and Roman Catholic Priests

Tineke Ferwerda

SCM PRESS LTD

Translated by John Bowden from *Zuster Philothea ziet gij nog niets komen...? Relaties tussen vrouwen en priesters*, published 1989 by Uitgeverij An Dekker, Amsterdam

© Tineke Ferwerda 1989

Translation © John Bowden 1993

334 01526 X

First British edition published 1993
by SCM Press Ltd,
26-30 Tottenham Road, London N1 4BZ

Phototypeset by Intype, London
and printed in Great Britain by
Mackays of Chatham, Kent

Abraxas is a god from Gnosticism who existed long before Christ.
He can be compared with the Christ of Atlantis; he is also known
under other names among the original inhabitants of North and
South America, for example among the Indians of my fatherland.
  Hermann Hesse speaks of him like this:

Look at the fire, look at the clouds, and immediately feelings arise
and voices begin to speak in your soul, and you give yourself to
them without first asking whether your father or your teacher or
another Dear Lord approves! This is the way in which people
destroy themselves. This is the way in which you get on to the
well-trodden path and become a fossil. Dear Sinclair, our God is
called Abraxas, he is God and he is Satan, he has both the light
and the dark world within him. Abraxas has nothing against
anything that happens in your thoughts or in your dreams. Don't
forget that. But he goes away from you if you ever become
bourgeois and normal. Then he goes away and looks for another
pot to cook his thoughts in.

M.Serano, *The Hermetic Circle*

Contents

Foreword

A book like this needs a foreword. But how can you write one if you keep quiet about all the things which women have told you in confidence?

Not many people know about them. Perhaps many women don't know that there are parallels between their love stories and the life stories of the 'Philothea sisters',[1] who have or have had the same problems in their relations with a priest.

If there is sisterhood, why shouldn't we support one another? That was the motivation for this investigation.

I realized when I placed the first advertisement on 31 January 1987 that I was taking a leap into space: space in two senses. On the one hand the space of the unknown, not knowing what you're going to find, and on the other hand the space which insight can create.

I had many reactions of different kinds from the Netherlands and Belgium, reactions in which I was told much that was personal and intimate. The problem is worldwide, but is not experienced everywhere to the same degree.

I never expected this investigation to become so intensive. My first advertisement brought 41 replies, and these were followed by another 110.

These reactions made me think about providing help. As a helper one often just stands there empty-handed: sometimes all you have to offer others is the possibility of being themselves. Your hope is that this moment can be the beginning of a positive change.

This book seeks to make space for words which are never, or hardly ever, spoken; to make space for the feelings of women who are having or have had a relationship with a Roman Catholic

1. Philothea means 'friend of God', see also pp.202, 205.

ix

priest. It seeks to provide some insight into these relationships: happy relationships in which both partners experience joy, but also relationships which bring sorrow and have trapped people, which have little to do with love as it is often presented to us by the church. Another aim of the book is to fight for space within the 'triumphalist Roman life'. I hope to find a listening ear and an open heart among those men concerned with obligatory celibacy. I hope that they can read what I have written without prejudice, without already having their verdict on the tip of their tongue. Let him who wants to cast the first stone first ask whether he himself is innocent.

I don't only want to describe the existing situation but also to provide an impulse towards change, a change which the women of priests can bring about in their own lives. I also want to bring about a change in the 'bystanders' which leads to more understanding.

Insight comes before change, and that's where I hope that this book will help.

It could not have been written without the contributions of all the women involved. Their stories and collaboration and the contributions by a number of priests form the basic nucleus.

I am extremely grateful, and hope that their stories can be a support for others.

Preface to the English edition

The first edition in another language. That's like standing on the quayside, waving good-bye to a ship going over the sea: a boat going into the unknown. At that point no one can say how it will fare; whether the voyage will be a safe one, with a good berthing and a warm welcome.

That the problem dealt with in this book is international has become even more evident from matters which have been given much publicity recently. There is already a long history between the origin of this book and the present moment, as I write these words for the English edition. As a result of reading the book, many women have undergone a process of growing awareness. They have been inspired and are offering themselves for group work or asking for individual help. A process of growth has started, and women are being motivated all at once to change their own situation for the better. Women with an existing relationship have found a better balance in it. They have gained more power over their own lives, rather than letting their priest friend determine it. They have also found more openness in their relationship. Some of them have registered their relationship officially, or have formalized as far as possible in the circumstances the duty of care that they feel towards one another. Women who once were the lovers of priests have been able to assimilate the pain of their broken relationship better and can begin something of a new life. Scars remain, but it is possible to deal with them meaningfully.

A women's network has formed, involving some of the women who took part in the investigation, related to the themes of the book. Meanwhile a good deal of experience has been gained and much has been learned about what must happen and what must not. Many women have been able to find a way to Philothea. One characteristic of the relationship with a priest is the secrecy, and the presupposition that you have to solve all the problems on your own. As the result of a book of this kind (that you can buy without having to talk about with anyone) and the follow-up provided by the Philothea network, women have found the possibility to break through the circle of isolation. Women from Philothea have now begun to set up a network in Belgium.

The Philothea network supports women who in one way or another have, or have had, problems through their relationship with a minister holding office in the Roman Catholic church. The church authorities still do not want to hear anything about this, even by providing financial help for all the work that is being done. Like much other work that is being done for women and by women, the work of Philothea is also an unpaid 'labour of love'. Charitable work, for women who are often cast aside by the church in a loveless way.

This edition contains (on p.202) a box number to which people can write for information, telling them, for example, how they can set up a network, how they can arrange group work, or edit a newsletter (but please enclose an international reply coupon!).

The final aim of this 'crossing' is that the women whom this book is about should determine their own course. I wish them a safe voyage.

8 March 1993, International Women's Day

Introduction

'Cultural ideals have a strong influence and give form not only to our way of thinking and acting but also to our way of being, to the conscious and unconscious content of our inner life. Moreover changes take place slowly and encounter enormous resistance in ourselves and in the system of social institutions which supports the rules of our society relating to femininity and masculinity – how a good wife lives, and how a good husband behaves.'

Lillian B.Rubin, *Intimate Strangers*

A completely new experience

'To begin with it was friendship. Later it became love. For him it was a completely new experience. An encounter with a woman who listened to him, a woman whom he could trust, with whom he could be open, be himself. He had really always been in search of the meaning of his existence. He intuitively felt that this meaning lay in everyday life itself. However, it was impossible for him to find personal confirmation of this. He was uncertain about his own existence, about the old norms and values, the old church. And also nostalgic for the certainties, when you were sure that you were doing good if you kept to them, though you might also say very modestly that you hadn't really been doing it very well. Life outside the old bastion was also attractive, full of new things, a love in which physical experience also became a delight. That was what the books were about: the excitement of a relationship which gives colour to the world around you. He could be in love like an adolescent, adoring the stars of heaven. But he drank a lot. Later that got worse and the division between illusion and reality became increasingly blurred. That made it even more difficult to see into the split within him.

"The most exciting thing is that I find in you a reflection of all my concerns. That's become so natural that it happens quite spontaneously. I feel that I can talk to you about anything." Words from his mouth. They sounded very honest and sincere. I was certain that we had a good relationship, very good. "Especially with you, it's good and safe, warm and intimate. Sometimes very deep and overwhelming, something that makes up my whole life. The exchange of our bodily warmth feels very harmonious. There too it's increasingly as if your body is mine, as if I've surmounted a division in which there is neither man nor woman but one whole person. Sometimes it feels very tender and vulnerable, as if you're touching the very nerves of life. You arouse longings in me to be an authentic person, whole and real... There's also something exciting in all the familiarity, something that looks forward, something that is sometimes sealed very deeply when we let ourselves flow out into each other, celebrating our love."

He often had the feeling that the church was no longer a home for him, that his brethren could not longer inspire him. Everything had become so ordinary in the church, so mediocre. He longed for the extraordinary, the eccentric, the mystical. There was little of that left. Nor could he be a bondservant of this church any more, since there was hardly any hierarchy left. Really he was constantly seeking the approval of others, to find in it the meaning of his existence before God. It was a tiring existence, always seeking affirmation afresh. It empties you, constantly looking for new inspiration: new things, other people, new places. Consequently it became evident that there were also other relationships. Safe relationships in which he could appear as comforter, as rescuer, which affirmed him. In which he again felt meaningful, able to direct the other. For me that was the end of our relationship. I could stand on my own feet and wanted to discover what life had to offer me and my partner in a monogamous relationship. Not to run away from any problems that might arise but to give an opportunity for growth in depth. "I want to grow old with you," he said once. But that never happened.

Shortly after we separated he took up a career in Ireland: it was again time to break off and burn his boats behind him, to begin all over again with a clean sheet. He kept up some contacts: it was easier by letter and more detached. He told many fibs and lies in our last period. He said that it was to protect me. He once invited me for a vacation in Paris. We had been there once before. When I didn't want to go again, he took a new girl friend with him. It was as interchangeable as that. Later I understood that it was the feeling of having lost face. He was constantly looking for affirmation.

When our relationship was over, so too was my faith. Our love had always had a religious dimension. We prayed together, and we felt that our love was a fragile flower given us by God.

It was not the fact that this love was over but his dishonesty, his twisting of the truth, that destroyed my faith. I thought that in him I had found a man who embodied my respect for the divine in everyone. That proved to be a bubble in the air. There was clearly no more left of our unique relationship which once delighted him so much than the position of a husband who can't get on with his wife, someone who is even in the first flush of a new relationship. My world caved in, and in retrospect I can say that this in itself taught me a great deal. Priests are just ordinary men, but the picture that we've formed of them during our relationship doesn't correspond to that. They give the impression of being able to deal so much better with people, of having so much more insight into what people can expect of one another: trust, loyalty and honesty. Now I know that it isn't my faith but the picture that I had formed of it, that has to collapse. It has to be killed off in order to grow into a more adult picture of God which is vulnerably present in everyone. It is no more present in a priest than, for example, in an architect, although the priest, supported by the church, gives us the idea that he has received more of God's grace. It's up to us how we experience 'God in us'.

All this doesn't have very much to do with faith. It has to do with the fact that you don't expect someone who says so many nice things about love, about living together as God's children, about loving your fellow human beings, to put so little of it into practice. You don't expect him still to be so illiterate in this field, because he has never really learned it. He has learned it all from books; he has learned that women are second-rate and that priests are superior to ordinary people. It is understandable that he determines what the relationship is going to look like, that he feels that everything must be subordinate to his work. If you want a man-woman relationship on equal terms, you will have to work hard for it. A good deal will have to be destroyed in him and also in you. You have to let him catch up on his adolescence. You have to revise your picture of this man who is no saint. You don't find it so easy to unlearn things that you learned in your youth. Some succeed. The priests with the gift of grace.

A priest who begins a loving relationship later in life has to catch up on all his adolescence, to discover all kinds of feelings about love. This sometimes produces an 'eclipse of God'. Sometimes you're still moved by adolescents; you think of the need to grow. A person wrestling with growth has the right to some compassion. He still has a good deal to learn. But I would rather not be involved in that. It's too easy to think that because one has a wide vocabulary one has already achieved adult loving. The reality can be a harsh one.

Women think too easily that the rose garden which their priest offers them in nice words is also reality. But he is simply making his own dream garden to escape into now and then, away from the hard world from which old certainties have disappeared. Often he finds a new certainty with you because you're an independent woman, because you don't really need him, because you aren't dependent on him. "You're the greatest person in my world and everything has become deeper and richer as a result. It's always more of what I've always dreamed of as real friendship." For him the difference between friendship and the love of man and woman often isn't clear, or he doesn't want to make it clear. Friendship is all right, but love between men and women is forbidden. So he will readily drop you, whereas you're ready to give yourself completely to the relationship. Women are also accustomed to giving themselves one hundred per cent to a relationship. We've learned that. But the meaning of his life has to lie in quite a different sphere.'

Everyone answers the question of the meaning of life in his or her own history

Women who have a relationship with a priest don't really exist. Priests need to live celibate lives, so according to official thinking they don't have any intimate relationships. If they do, then for most, but not for all, it is in the utmost secrecy.

> 'Of course after a long argument, my partner and I decided to cut the knot, in favour of our secret relationship. This secrecy no longer made sense to me. I told anyone who wanted to listen that we loved one another and that I was not the housekeeper. The telephone never stopped, bringing calls telling me that I was a "slut" and a "whore". My partner was disowned by his parents and some of his brothers. There were five hundred signatures on a petition to drive us out of the village. Charges like "immorality with children" and "they have a child" came to the bishop's ear. At that time it was still Bishop X, a fine man. In the end we stood firm and we're still in our village. Now we're only a few years from retirement. How incredibly stupid religion is!'

Reality shows that there are indeed relationships between women and priests, happy ones and unhappy ones, as there are between people everywhere. There are relationships in which people experience lifelong joy and from which they draw strength to face problems. There are also relationships in which people are unhappy. Or relationships which are broken off but leave sorrow behind for a long time afterwards.

> 'It's now sixteen years since it happened, and I'm fifty-nine. But four years of your life isn't nothing: the love for each other, the sorrow as well, and the joy, but always all that secrecy, your guilt feelings: it may not be, it cannot be.'

Why do many women continue to be accomplices in 'that secrecy'? Why do women feel guilty? Because society tells them to, or because the partner runs the risk of losing his job for having a relationship? Or does it lie much deeper?

'It is important that society and church should recognize these friendships and forms of living together, resulting in all the rights and duties which are to be found in our society at this moment. This is possible if we stop making them sensations at which outsiders chuckle and to which the church authorities react with great fear and opposition. I want this subject to be treated properly. Friendship and trust between people are the best things in life. If people can provide this, sometimes despite pain, it is worth respect.'

We live in a time of disclosures, and many tabus have already been broken. Things which once barely seemed to exist are now coming into the daylight. They are being looked at again and interpreted by people whom they concern personally. Many of these people have the courage to replace the old negative label with a new honest interpretation. They tell us how it really is, because they are involved heart and soul. Many of these people are women, women who keep quiet because that is what they were taught, because that was seemly; because the stories which they had to tell didn't match the picture that people, usually from the male half of society, had of reality. In this book a group of women have their say, women who have or have had a relationship with a priest. They want to become visible; they want their stories to be heard. They want to share their experiences with others. Once they begin to talk, their story doesn't seem as unique as they thought, nor are their problems as private as they had supposed. Talking about them with others provides new perspectives.

'It is most important for me to share experiences. To reflect with others on the background. How you make clear that these relationships indeed exist. For me, another aim of the exchange of experiences is to support one another and make one another more resistant. It's very difficult on your own.'
'I think it's extremely important for people to write about this tabu. The hypocritical thought of many priests often comes out more clearly in a relationship. I hope that we can help one another.'

Some of us wisely keep quiet. Others live imprisoned with their secret, their sorrow or their child. Sometimes with bitterness, sometimes without looking round in anger. There are women who tell all, who want openness. Some lead a happy life, sometimes only after years. Others feel the consequences for their partner – resignation or expulsion from the priesthood.

Choices are possible: to opt for a relationship without sex, to be resigned to not being the wife of your partner, or to stop because the relationship is too painful.

This book gives some idea of how women experience a relationship with a priest. Women express themselves here through the results of a questionnaire to twenty-three of them and the roughly one hundred reactions which I got. Then there are also the life-stories of the women themselves. Sometimes these are very long, extending over twenty years of their lives. Sometimes they are very short, with fragments from their lives. Here are stories with women in the foreground. Then on the horizon there appears a picture of the priest who enters into such a relationship. These priests themselves have their say. Some of them wanted to get their story off their chests. They thought it important that women and society should hear something of their own experiences, because they often suffer from the same secrecy, the same stigmas.

'My friend and I have both gone through all kinds of stages of anxieties, secrets and frustrations, each from our own past. And yet we never completely get rid of our past. Rest only came when we realized that something good had happened to us and that that was our strength. We had to learn to accept that along with all that was possible and all that was impossible, and then we could be happy with it.'

The questionnaire and the reactions to it showed that many problems arise in the relationship with a priest. These are partly caused by the fact that he is a priest, and partly because the magic words 'I love you' seem to women to be the promise of a happy life: *seem* to be, because it so often turns out otherwise. You slowly come to realize that you're keeping back much of yourself, not letting it come to the surface because it's such a burden for him. You've learned from your upbringing that as a woman you may not put yourself too much in the foreground, that you have to serve.

'I swallowed a good deal; my priority was the passionate wish that he should be happy. Yes, a woman can bear a great deal.'

Perhaps you bear a good deal because of him. Are you yourself happy? If that is the case, then I congratulate you. If it isn't, then it's high time to see why. Can something be changed, can you change anything in yourself so that the relationship also contributes to your happiness? If your relationship has been broken off, it may be that you are still always in pain because perhaps you've never been able to talk about it with anyone, because you've never been able to understand why it was like this.

'I too have been the victim of such a relationship with a priest. At the time I was no wiser, but this period still weighs heavy on my conscience. It still nauseates me. If they're afraid of losing their good reputation, you're pushed aside as a whore. It has nothing whatsoever to do with love, but with self-importance, with passion. I've never been able to talk about it with anyone.'

The first women who had been involved in my investigation wanted to meet to talk about their existing or broken relationships. That happened at various times. It led to a network. This book is also about that: can women help one another by exchanging experiences? Can there be more understanding as a result of women making their experiences better known?

Finally, this is also a matter of gearing, as in cycling. If you use a low gear you pedal faster, but it's easier; you don't go as fast as you do in top gear, but it's much easier to get up hills. To my mind you often need such low gearing to oppose the view 'What's all the fuss about?', to resist a false picture of reality.

A bishop recently said in a radio interview: 'That doesn't happen in my diocese.' For anyone who thinks that all priests live celibate lives, the women who have taken part in the questionnaire and those who have responded to the publicity over it have another story: their own story, in which many things are told, intimate things. They tell of their happiness but also of their sorrow; their frustrations over the church and over the influence which the patriarchal structures have had on their lives. Sometimes they describe how they've wrestled with their faith, a faith which often disappeared the moment the relationship collapsed – as the *coup de grâce*. They had often already had difficulties with the patriarchal forms in the church.

The decree *Ad hominem*

The American Roman Catholic professor of theology Rosemary Radford Ruether wrote an article which begins like this: 'Recently a synod of bishops and a large number of general superiors met in the Holy City for a solemn session, to take action on the much-discussed question of whether men should be admitted to the ministry.'

She goes on to describe the course of the session. The synod came to the conclusion that men are unsuited for the ministry because of their gender, that they are above all suited to doing the heavier work, like digging ditches and repairing roofs. Our Mother in heaven has reserved the finer, more spiritual, tasks for those with a more refined mind and body, women. We also see this division in scripture, where it is said that men are made of the dust whereas women are created from human tissue. Moreover woman was created last, and that clearly stamps her as the crown of God's creation. One mother superior even remarked that Adam was a rough model and that Eve was the more refined and complete version of the physical person. The mothers laughed heartily at this and some planned to make the text a car-bumper sticker.

From questionnaire to dissertation to book

My work has already involved me for a number of years in women's welfare. From my position as a woman in society (marriage – family – work – church – society) I have come to see that women regard many questions and problems as personal matters, whereas these often have a social context. Girls are socialized to be nice gentle women with a great capacity for empathy. Many of us already found the blueprint for our roles in the cradle. Fortunately, a large number of women are now asking themselves whether they are really content with this role and the social expectations that go with it. They are reflecting on it and think it worth fighting for a better future. In all kinds of spheres women are discovering their own strength and making themselves heard: black women, white women, social aid women, women with an academic training, professional women, housewives, mothers, widows, young girls, worldly women, nuns and prostitutes.

Because they have kept silent for too long...

Because they have been drowned out for too long...

Those were enough reasons for me to immerse myself in the roles and backgrounds of women. But why in those of the women of priests? I suspected that this group of women might be greater than could be assumed. My own experience, a chance (?) contact with another woman, was the beginning of a first cautious investigation. That became a dissertation on a group of women who felt a problem and wanted to do something about it, women who wanted to overcome a problem which is as old as celibacy. Perhaps it has not happened very often that any large number of women themselves have wanted to say anything about it. But nowadays women no longer so readily make their interests subordinate to those of men. In this respect we are up with the times. In another respect we are against the times: as a result of the stubborn attitude of the church hierarchy, people have to act more secretly about their relationships than in the 1960s. In this book, all women who are directly involved can now read what other women feel about their relationship and how they deal with the problems that can arise from it. The disadvantage is that it may bring out things that provoke new prejudices. This can have repercussions, make people angry, or wound them, because it goes against the picture that they have aways had of the church and of priests. Perhaps some people simply don't want to believe these stories because some of them sound incredible. But they have all happened; they are not fairy tales.

For *whom is this book intended?*

In the first place I want to address women themselves, the 'Philothea sisters'. I want to call them 'women in the same situation'; I'm deliberately not saying that they share the same fate. That sounds irrevocable, as if your fate is something that you cannot change, but which you must endure. That's not the case. I want to make clear what you yourself can do – provided that you want to and dare to. But you have to dare.

This book can help the 'brothers' – partners of women –, superiors and bishops to a better understanding of the shepherds and the flock. This could lead to an attitude which does justice to people, as a result of which they can lead happier lives.

It emerges from the stories of women and from the literature that many priests also find their situation oppressive. The choice of celibacy was made at the end of their studies, around the age of twenty-five, for the rest of their lives. Sometimes personal growth and a better insight into life has led them to regret this choice. The women in this book have met men who for one reason or another have broken their vows of celibacy. I have also made room for the stories of some of these priests, to give an idea of how this vow gets broken. They too have their own stories.

Women certainly approach counselling agencies to ask for help and advice about their relationships with priests:

> 'We are regularly rung up by women who describe their experiences with a priest who wants to enter into a sexual relationship under the guise of help' (Women against Sexual Abuse from Welfare Workers).

> 'In recent years I've had quite a lot of contact with people who have been sexually abused by a priest, a monk or a nun' (a psychotherapist).

I also want to make a contribution to the counselling of women. So it is important to indicate for whom this book is meant. I would want to say that it is written from a feminist perspective. However, 'feminist perspective' still has negative connotations. So I shall explain what I mean here.

The feminist model emphasizes the difference in power between men and women, the oppressive patterns and mechanisms, and the social surroundings of women themselves. Here is what was said about this at a study day of the Women's Support Group in The Hague:

'To be powerless means that a woman must always be on the alert about the reactions of those with power and that she must adapt to them in order to be able to function. It means that the powerless must be able to develop a number of characteristics in order to survive. Women are made to reflect on what the powerful think, feel and want, and to adjust their actions to this. This view casts quite a different light on the much-praised feminine intuition. On the other hand, to be powerful means that a person does not have to be steeped in what the other feels, thinks or wants. Regardless of what it means for the other person, someone can control him or her.'

Within the feminist support group, knowledge of socialization and social position is used in approaching problems.

Theories and methods are aimed at gaining insight into social relationships. In order to be able to function within these relationships, each person develops particular patterns of behaviour. Considerable parallels can be discovered between women in particular patterns, as for example being loving, sweet and understanding, not being angry, making oneself unobtrusive, thinking ill of oneself and good of others, being afraid of power and independence. These are patterns which restrict the personal development of women. Within the feminist support group work has been done on seeing which patterns are good and which are restrictive. In the light of this, work has also been done on getting more of a grip on individual life, learning to make deliberate choices and gaining confidence in one's own thought and power. The most important phrases in the feminist support group are: becoming aware, recognition, social understanding, personal insight, self-discovery, being yourself, finding strength.

Feminism is concerned with a process of liberating women so that they become independent. There are two sides to this process: a personal side like achieving self-awareness as a woman so that others cannot gain power over one's person, and a political and social side, like standing up together for equal opportunities and equal rights for women.

The start of the investigation

In order to discover whether there were women who had a relationship with a priest and what they felt about it, on 31 January 1987 I put an advertisement in a number of Dutch newspapers, both Catholic and Protestant, with the following text, which also gave a box number.

> In connection with personal experience for a dissertation in Social Studies I would like reactions (anonymous) from women who have (or have had) a relationship with a Roman Catholic priest.

There was now an opening. Everyone knew that there were such relationships between women and Roman Catholic priests. You only had to listen to the gossip about the priest and his house-keeper. But was a woman-priest relationship frequent? And were women prepared to say anything about it? Did such a relationship pose specific problems? If so, how did women deal with them? I found the reactions to the advertisement sufficient encouragement to pursue my investigation into the form and content of these relationships and whether or not there were signs that this was a social problem, and to study how women sought a solution to these problems. Can we help one another, learn from one another? Can we also see these problems in a social context? What kind of relationships are these? Is there a common factor in them other than the mere fact that the partner is a priest? Do they differ from the relationships of women whose partner is, for example, a baker? Meanwhile I had already seen and experienced several cases at close range. I listened to many stories, including the stories of priests. Through interested parties I obtained literature from abroad, particularly from Germany. In it I found the stories of women, but no indications of possibilities for change. So I went further and became aware that I would be involved in an unorthodox investigation of an unorthodox subject.

Taking as my starting point the direct experience of women

13

and how their ideas had been shaped, I wanted to try to find the common element in these relationships. What problems do women indicate and what do they do about them? Can these problems be overcome? If so, how? What can we learn from the women's support organizations and from feminist literature?

My aim was to gain insight into the relationships which women have with priests. I established that three questions were central to my investigation:

(i) What do women feel about a relationship with a priest?
(ii) Are there specific problems?
(iii) If so, what can you do about them?

I drafted a questionnaire to get an answer to the first question.

What does such a relationship look like on the basis of an analysis of the problem through a questionnaire? What elements does such a relationship consist of, what kind of influence does it have on the woman/partner of a priest? What aspects have a negative and what aspects have a positive aspect for the relationship?

To answer the second question, I looked for common features in the answers to the questionnaire and began to compare them with facts that I encountered in the literature. After that, to answer the third question I began to examine the methods of support to see what possibilites there were of altering the situation.

There was a great diversity of answers. There were also common features. With the information that I gathered from the questionnaire I organized group meetings.

The questionnaire

When framing the questions I was guided by the information I had acquired through the responses to my advertisement, both verbal and written, and by facts from the literature. The answers were to show that the specific problems were similar.

An investigation like this does not claim to be complete, nor does it aim to present firm figures. Rather, it is meant to bring out agreements and differences.

I am aware that the responses to the advertisement are themselves a selection. However, at this moment I see no other way of arriving at facts.

The questions in the questionnaire were framed in such a way as to illuminate the questions that I asked myself. From the answers I examined the theory.

Identification

On a separate sheet, as a supplement to the questionnaire which I sent out, women could indicate whether they wanted to meet a number of other women who were in a similar situation. I asked this question because my first contact indicated that such a meeting and exchange seemed to make sense.

This had already taken place in miniature. I had a meeting with three women – on a completely different issue – who were very interested in my investigation. They made contact with one another to discuss their relationships and found it useful to exchange experiences.

After working through the questionnaire I attempted to organize meetings for women whose experiences had been predominantly positive and women whose experiences had been predominantly negative. The colouring of the experience was indicated by the women themselves. The questionnaire illuminated the relationships. The meetings confirmed the facts that I had gathered from the questionnaire. Here were two sources to draw on. The story of anyone who is having or has had such a relationship provides quite a distinctive picture. So this book also consists of stories by women and priests about their relationship. The stories of the women come first. Second come the stories of some priests who are still in office. There is the story of a priest who has left the priesthood and that of a priest who tells his story on the point of leaving. His woman friend, his bride-to-be, also tells her story. Then there are the roughly one hundred letters from women who had heard of the investigation through publicity about it. Not only women who were having (or who had had) a relationship with a priest, but also priests and helpers:

'Of the 3,500 priests in the Netherlands, some dozens, perhaps a hundred, have had problems [with celibacy], but these figures are no more than a guess' (Cardinal Simonis in an interview, 9 January 1989).

A guess. Simonis is right to say this. From my own investigation and from the letters which I received afterwards, I too would estimate around a hundred. But were all the relationships 'reported'? The most important aspect of a relationship with a priest is that it is secret. It is illogical to presuppose that all those involved would make such a relationship known on the basis of a small advertisement or some publicity about the existence of such relationships. Often major interests are at stake. Moreover, my aim is not to prove that priests do not lead celibate lives; there are many priests who certainly do. That is unimportant within the framework of this book. What is more important is that there are women – more than we thought at first – who have a relationship with a priest and want to make it better and avoid the difficulties that they find in it. It is also more important that there are women who have had these sad experiences with a priest, but have never, or hardly ever, been able to talk about them, and have suffered distress over them for years.

Perhaps now we should let the women speak first. Women who have had a relationship with a priest, who have been happy, but have also had the burden of secrecy. Women who have not had such good experiences, women who are sad, angry, in a crisis over their faith, or who no longer want to have anything to do with the church. After their stories I shall try to see how this has come about, what has led to it, what the causes have been. And finally, what can be done about it.

Heaven and hell

There is an ancient Hasidic story about the rabbi who spoke with the Lord about heaven and hell. 'I shall show you hell,' said the Lord, and he put the rabbi in a chamber in the middle of which there was a very big, round table. The people who sat round it were hungry and despairing. In the middle of the table was a large pan with a stew, enough for everyone. The smell made the rabbi's mouth water. Each of the people round the table had a spoon with an enormously long handle. They could reach the pan, but because the handles were longer than their arms, they could not put the spoons to their mouths. The rabbi saw how terrible this was for them. 'Now I shall show you heaven,' said the Lord, and they went into another room. There was the same table and the same pan with the stew. The people had the same spoons wth long handles, but they looked happy and well-fed and strong; they laughed and talked. At first the rabbi didn't understand. 'It's quite simple,' said the Lord, 'but there is something you need to know. They've learned to feed each other.'

from Irvin D. Yalom, *Group Therapy in Theory and Practice*

The story of Adam and Eve

There follows the life-story of Eve, into which Adam makes his entrance at a certain point. They both tell how their relationship came about and how they dealt with their problems, what they felt about their love and what it means for them to go through life together.

Eve was born in the war, in 1942, the third child of a family with four children. Her mother was forty, her father thirty-four: simple, believing, religious people who observed God's commandments as given them by the Roman Catholic church.

'As was usual at that time, we were actively involved in church activities. We went to Holy Mass and Benediction and joined in processions. My father went on retreat every year and took part in the famous annual procession in Amsterdam. I liked church activities because of the warm atmosphere, the light, and being together with so many people.

I also thought it great that we did this as a family. My mother was the one who taught us to pray and sing hymns. We did that a lot, above all when things were difficult. Particularly when my father had an attack. He was epileptic. Such an attack was terrible to see, but also worrying, because then he was unconscious for hours. My mother would sit with him and we had to pray for him to come round. It seemed as though this depended on our praying hard – otherwise it wouldn't happen. That was a great burden for us. I felt that I was under enormous pressure. His state of health was also a reason for keeping us in check, since when we became too obstreperous my father got cross and then he could have an attack. In addition, my mother had migraines every month, which was another reason for keeping quiet.

In our family we always prayed with a fixed number of

intentions: in honour of St Cornelius, the patron of people with epilepsy, and of St Joseph for work (my father was often unemployed because of his illness). There were also prayers for priestly vocations, for lapsed priests, for priests who had died, for people behind the Iron Curtain and those who were persecuted. A whole scale. And there were novenas when there were difficult situations in our family, with our relations or our circle of friends. My parents were convinced that we belonged to the One True Church. We weren't allowed to play at home with other children if their parents were lapsed Catholics. Out of doors we did play with these children. And once I also took my friend to church. I was proud of everything that we had in the church. My parents were always very devout and I thought it impressive to see how intensely they prayed, each in their own way. They showed us that God is someone to whom you can say anything and who gives you strength when things are difficult. You have to be quiet to hear what God is telling you. Above all we had to listen to our parents and they in turn had to listen to God, who was their master. For us that came later, when we had grown up. It was a kind of hierarchy which I found good.

As a child I already had difficulty with my parents' attitude to the 'lapsed' and those of 'other persuasions'. I couldn't make this fit with what they said about God who was good to all people and even had dealings with sinners. I disobeyed my parents and began to play with my friends at home. I then felt guilty because I really shouldn't. I didn't dare say 'I'm ashamed of my parents'. When my mother asked were I'd been, I told her a fib. Later I confessed that and my little lie was forbidden. But it kept coming back: there was no real solution. My parents always spoke with respect of the clergy. If they heard something negative they said that clergy, too, were human and that it must be very difficult to be alone and not to have a family.'

When I asked her about her sexual upbringing she told me this:

'Sex was a very secret matter. My mother told me that I mustn't touch my body in some places. That was forbidden, that was bad. "You'll catch something from it." I always had to sit "nicely" with my legs together: "You'll make men think funny thoughts."

I was not to romp with boys and they were not to feel up my skirt. My girl friend and I once went for a walk with a neighbour's baby in a pram. I thought that it would be very exciting to see whether this baby had a clean nappy. I found the penis, or if it was a girl the labia, nice to look at. I felt that this was really wrong, but the excitement that I felt won over the prohibition. With friends we often played "fathers and mothers". We then found it necessary to look at one another and touch one another. When my mother later asked what we had been doing my face went red. She then said: "Remember, even if I don't see it, God sees you, always and everywhere. You can't hide anything from him. He's watching you when you tell fibs." If you did something you shouldn't, then our Dear Lord got cross and that mustn't happen since he would punish you in one way or another.

I was also warned that I mustn't flirt with men, because then they would want "something" and that wasn't allowed. When I asked what this "something" was, my mother got cross and said: "Keep your mouth shut, you must listen to what your mother says. Do you understand?" Then I felt really awful, a mixture of anger and helplessness. I loved my mother and couldn't bear it when she was cross with me. When we went away with girl friends my mother said very emphatically that we mustn't go with strange men; they were child molesters. "If you go with them, perhaps you'll never come back, or they'll hurt you."

Since our home was small and you could hear everything that went on, I heard when my parents had quarrels. Usually they were over sex. My father wanted it often, and my mother wasn't always in the mood. She would refuse my father, as people called it at the time. My father thought that he had the right to it: my mother had to do her duty. If she didn't, then she was guilty if my father sinned. He mightn't lose any seed, i.e. not even masturbate. He would then threaten to "go to other women who want to do it". He also said that it would be her fault if he violated his daughters. I remember very well that there were often rows about this. As a child I felt very anxious when I was alone with my father. That was above all because I had witnessed one of his epileptic attacks. I saw him sprawling with foam on his lips. He seemed like a beast. He also drowned kittens as though it were nothing. And even large cats which sat in our garden and got fish out of his pond. Seeing him skin our rabbit around Easter was also too much for my childish soul. I found this quite horrible. I often thought to myself as he sat next to me: one day he'll also drown me.

In past years I've discovered that I was also afraid of my father because he couldn't control the anger that flowed out of him. In the last phase of his life we were able to talk about that. He cried when he told me how anxious he had been that he might violate me or my sister. Then I asked him whether that had ever happened. His answer was: 'Fortunately not, but I was always afraid of it. Your mother often didn't want sex and my body kept asking for it.' When we had discussed this it became clear to me where my anxiety about him came from: I always felt threatened by something unknown.

Around my twelfth birthday I got curious about the penises of big boys. My brother, who was two years older, usually went to bed with me at the same time. I was always troubled with cold feet and I once asked him whether I could warm my feet on him. He said yes, so I crept into bed with him. As well as wanting to warm my feet, I found it marvellous to feel his warm body. Of course I touched his penis. I found that very exciting. After a while I had to get out of his bed. I was aware that this must be a sin, so I asked God for forgiveness. I did this straightaway in bed. But then I repeatedly got out again and always with the same course. I also went to confession, and said that I had done something that my father and mother mustn't see. Fortunately no priest ever went into it. The first time I was terribly anxious about it. But I had to go to confession, otherwise I would go to hell.

At this time my mother thought that we were too old to sleep together in one room. You could never know whether something would happen between us, and she didn't want that on her conscience. My oldest brother moved into the loft and I slept with my sister in a double bed. I found it marvellous to lie with her; she was always very warm. My mother once tried to warn my sister and me. When she started to talk, we both burst out laughing, since we already knew it all. She got cross and said that street talk wasn't good, that we didn't need to know it if we didn't want to listen. Later I thought it a shame for her; who knows how difficult it had been for her to get that far?

When I was fourteen I went to work. I was allowed to keep the money I earned, but I had to pay for my own clothes. I thought that this was fantastic and felt that I was grown-up. Before that I had been put in a kind of transitional grade, but after some months I had to leave because my parents were working-class and couldn't afford to pay for me to study. I went to work in a guest-house which belonged to a hospital; the same group of religious cared for the guests and the sick. There had also been sisters at school, and I thought it great to be working with them. It was always relaxed there and I could go to chapel. The atmosphere of prayer attracted me, and it was a protected environment. When I was fifteen, I went on holiday to visit a pen-friend. On the way to the station I was accosted by a man. He wanted to take me to a "great place" where we would do "nice things". In a flash all my mother's warnings returned. He was on a bicycle and I was walking with a case and a bag. I was terribly anxious. He used words that I didn't know and kept pursuing me on his bicycle. Suddenly he pedalled away. I saw a police car coming. I stood as though nailed to the ground and sadly didn't think of stopping the police car. During my week's holiday this man kept going through my head. This put me off the family I was staying with and I thought up a lie to go home. Because my mother had written me a letter, I told them that my father was sick and I wanted to go home. When I got home I said that there were fleas in the house, but I don't know whether I said anything about that funny man. It wouldn't surprise me if I didn't. My mother would then have warned me all over again. The problem was that she was always right, and I found that exhausting.

Some time later I was molested by one of the guests at the guest-house. He touched me on my budding breasts. I felt deeply offended. At the time I cried a lot. I was seen by the head of the guest house, an understanding, wise woman. I also had to go to the superior to tell her what had happened. Her reaction was that she came into contact with this a lot. Men were like that, they were weak and couldn't help it. I was very timid after this conversation. Later I was shocked by an old man going along with his penis hanging out of his trousers. I thought that nauseating and resolved never to marry. I didn't feel like having to cope with these funny men. Sex became a real evil as far as I was concerned.

I did also come into contact with nice boys and men, but I always kept an eye on them if they got fresh. You never knew what they might do. Drunk men were unsavoury; they slobbered and had funny conversations. I realized that my father was also a man and so he too could do these strange things. I found that creepy. Perhaps my mother was right. But of course there had to be children, otherwise the world would be empty. The more the children, the greater the praise of God, and that was what life was about – at least that's what my mother had told me. People are on earth to serve God and if you do that you can be happy here on earth and in the hereafter. That was a kind of fate that you couldn't escape.

When my older sister had a boy-friend my mother got upset. My father thought it quite natural. My mother threatened to drown herself if my sister went to see her boy-friend. I was terribly afraid that she really would do this and said that I would go with her – she already had her coat on. I then went for a walk with her. The comic thing was that I saw my sister and her boy-friend walking about fifty yards away. My mother was so cross and upset that she saw nothing.

At dances I noted that I kept boys at a distance because I was afraid of them. I felt safer when I was in the guest-house. Often I went to the sisters' prayers and felt increasingly attracted to them. In 1958 a friend became a religious. I went to visit her. It was a splendid atmosphere. In 1959 I began to think of becoming a religious, too. I remember that during an introductory conversation I hoped deep within myself that someone would explore my reasons for making this choice so that all my bottled-up anxieties and sorrow could come to the surface. But unfortunately this didn't happen, so I resolved to become a religious. Far from the narrow world of men, who always had something dirty in mind, who always thought of their own enjoyment. To live only for God was the best thing that I could do. With God I was at least safe and I could pray for all these other people with problems. Moreover, in the meantime my godfather had left his wife and was living with another woman. That was a scandal for the family. But my parents helped him and encouraged us to visit this uncle and the aunt who had suddenly appeared. In a short space of time they had two children. I had gone into retreat to reflect on whether I indeed had a vocation. I had read various things about how you could know whether you had a vocation. The only indication that I could use as a sign of vocation was that I should offer a kind of debt of honour to God for the sins of my godfather. I left everything behind me and went into the convent to live for God. I was convinced that this was my way of life.

I entered in 1960. I had needed my parents' consent for this. When I told them that I wanted to go into the convent they both thought this a good thing. They had always prayed that a son should become a priest and a daughter go into the convent. On the one hand I was glad that they approved, but on the other I asked myself whether they really loved me, since they gave their consent so easily. After that I devoted myself wholly to life in the convent: what I liked best were the choir offices, the singing lessons and the biblical exposition. I had gained my diploma in religion at this time and also had lessons in general formation. At the time I had to work very hard, and we had to make shoes according to extremely strict rules. After six months I was invested, i.e. received a habit from the congregation and took another name. This was a symbol of the new life that had begun, detached from what you had been before. You could choose a name, but if the superior didn't like it, you had to choose another. That's what happened to me: I had to choose the name of a sister who lay dying, because I was to be the same type. That would be the only name which fitted me. I found this a bit much. I could live just as well before God with the name that my parents had given me. There were many customs in the convent connected with humbling yourself, making yourself smaller so that God constantly became greater. "It is not I who live, but God lives in me." As for sexuality, I just noticed that three sisters were always together as much as possible. At one particular time two of them were found together in bed. We knew that because we slept in open rooms, cells. So you heard everything. The two were betrayed by someone, and soon afterwards they left.

In October 1962 I made my provisional vows: in them you promised to live in obedience, poverty and chastity for a year. On 4 November 1962, along with two of my group, I was moved to the community in X. This was a group of 112 religious, with an age-range of between twenty and eighty-six. I was put to work in the hospital laundry, where three religious, two launderers and about fifteen women were working. I heard things from these women which made me blush, but fortunately I kept quiet about them. It became clear to me that sex played a major part in human life. One of the other sisters had a good deal of difficulty with the fact that I was so popular with the personnel. She lost no opportunity to torment me. As a young sister I could do nothing about it.

In 1963 I began to train as a nurse. While washing a patient who was lying flat in bed with traction on his skull, I was for the first time confronted with someone getting an erection from my touch. I had to escape, so I decided to put a cloth on his penis and go away. That didn't help, so I went on washing him and dressing him. The man didn't know what to do either. The only thing I said was that it would be better for someone else to look after him. He thoroughly agreed. Afterwards, this situation seemed to have made a bond between us: we had good conversations with each other.

Before I made my permanent vow, I fell in love with an assistant and he with me. He often sought me out when I had night duty: we had much to talk about over the patients. At one particular moment he asked whether I wanted to stay in the convent. I told him that I would be making my final profession at the end of the year. We both laughed quite a lot about that – I think out of nerves. For weeks I had difficulties, because I loved him, but also wanted to remain faithful to the choice of the convent that I had made earlier. When I was convinced that I had to stick to that I told him that I wanted to put an end to our contacts because I found them difficult. He respected that. In the three years of my provisional vows I had several times doubted whether I should make my final vows. When I talked about this to my spiritual director or confessor I got the following reaction: "That's the devil, that's a temptation. The devil doesn't want you to give yourself to God. Conquer this temptation and you'll become all the stronger, and then you'll certainly know that this is your vocation." I often worried about this. At one particular moment I said that I would indeed make my final vows, because they were in a better position to judge than I was. And that is what I did in 1965.

In 1968 I fell ill. In my view this was because of the pest of a head sister and severe pressure from family problems. People seem to think that if you're a religious you can do anything. I heard that from everyone around, but I didn't hear whether there was a solution. Nobody gave me any personal counselling; they spoke only about my work. My parents were having many difficulties at this time. My mother wrote me long letters about her sexual problems. Sometimes I didn't even know what some of the words meant, let alone having any solution. All that I had to offer was to pray for her, and I told her that.

I had a hormone imbalance and that made me physically and mentally out of balance. The sisters and my family lavished much care on me, but there was just no one to whom I could talk about my spiritual problems. After seventeen weeks in hospital I was discharged. I immediately went to a smaller group which in the meantime had been formed from the community of 112. That was in 1967. We wore ordinary clothes. We wanted to live among people in an ordinary way and have real contact with one another. This need emerged from discussion groups and within the community, where we observed that we scarcely knew one another. It had always been long and hard work. A couple of periods of recreation with compulsory craftwork was not enough to create a sense of community. I went to live in a group of seven people. For the first months I stayed at home, but after that I began to work one hour a day. After a year I was working five hours a day. Meanwhile I had started to work with the handicapped – I was twenty-six.

I had a good bond with a fellow-sister. We quickly got to know one another and had the same interests. One lunchtime we went for a walk and she suddenly said, "You can't expect any more of me." I was amazed and responded, "What more do you think that I expect of you? I want our contact to remain as it is, we get on well and have a great friendship." "That's good," she replied.

26

When we got home she embraced me so warmly that I felt uncomfortable. "Thank you," she said. I didn't understand. Our relationship continued to remain good until we got into another group. Contact diminished. Once again I felt that sex had something to do with it. One of the sisters had a special relationship with another sister. I thought this a somewhat cloying relationship. No one could come in between. When the oldest wasn't there, for the moment someone else was the closest. When the older person came back, the other was forgotten. There was also a special atmosphere at bed-time. Once I was visited by this person in my room. She suddenly bent over me and began to kiss me passionately. I didn't know what to do. I felt attacked and pushed her away. I felt as though I had been raped. After that I was afraid of her, because she wanted things that I didn't.

In 1975 Adam came to the parish as pastor. I met him at a celebration of the liturgy. I found him attractive and thought that he might find it difficult in the parish. He didn't live in the clergy house but by himself. I and another sister began to visit him. I thought that he had set up his home very well. I hoped that he wouldn't be lonely; that would be a shame for such a fine young man. We often had contact with each other and I felt at ease with him. I got the impression that he was a homosexual from the way he walked and dressed and from his sensitivity. I thought it good that there were also men with whom you could have contact without them beginning to make passes at you.

During a retreat the leader fell in love with me. I also found him charming, felt attracted to him. He was always in the same group during recreation at the end of the day. On one particular occasion he asked if he could dance with me. He also did this with other sisters, but he came for me often. I noticed that I was aroused when he touched me. At the end of the evening he asked another sister and me to go to his room. We chatted a bit. I found that very exciting. Suddenly he stood up, gave me a kiss, and said: 'Do you know that I like you a lot? Yesterday evening I wrote something about tenderness. I felt that you inspired it.' I was amazed and also happy. That night I didn't sleep much. Questions went though my head: What was I to do? What did it all mean? The next evening we danced again. Later, when we were alone,

27

he took me in his arms. We kissed each other for a long time. It seemed as if all my hidden feelings were coming to the surface. I had to get a grip of myself. I really wanted to go with him to his room. My longing for intimate contact was very strong. I reflected that I was a religious and couldn't allow myself anything like this. This experience made me ask again whether I was really suited to remaining a religious. It was a cold life. Now I had had another experience and knew that warmth was also possible.

These and other situations made me begin to wonder about my choice of life. I was convinced that I could also live as a good Christian outside the convent. In the course of time and in discussion with others, I decided to leave the group and live in rooms. Alone, I would be able to come back to myself. I felt alienated from myself, I was submerged in the group, I no longer had any personality. I had told Adam my plans. He promised to help me to move. I enjoyed the freedom which came from living alone. I found it splendid not to have to give an account of what I had done or where I had been, and no longer to be told that I had got back too late.

On Friday evenings I went to Adam's house. I wanted to use his shower, since I didn't have one. Usually he wasn't at home when I came. After a few weeks I waited for him in the evening. Then we chatted for a bit before I went home. I lived about ten minutes away. One evening we were listening to music and I invited him to dance. He hesitated, but did. We danced on other occasions and I began to feel more for him.

I continued to long increasingly for a partner in life and resolved to leave the order. In 1978 I did so. That was a very emotional event in my life.

Two weeks after I left, I proved to have a tumour in my stomach. The gynaecologist asked whether I still wanted children. If I did, he would carry out a rescue operation if possible. My relationship with Adam was still in its early stages. I didn't know whether I would ever enter into another relationship. I resolved not to have my womb removed if there were any possibility of keeping it. It was a tense situation. Adam showed much understanding and was a good listener to my uncertainties. He often came to visit me in hospital. When I got home again, I expected him but had to wait for him for several days. When he came, I told him of my disappointment. He didn't understand and said he had no obligations to me. This remark made me sad.

By 1980 the relationship had already grown a lot. Adam let me know now and then that he didn't want any ongoing relationship with me. I mustn't lay claim to him either.

When a friend of his fell sick and died, we talked a lot. When he got back from the funeral we embraced each other. That was a very intense experience for both of us. Suddenly Adam broke away, as if I had a contagious disease. I was struck dumb. Obviously it was difficult for him to show his emotions.

When I went for a shower a couple of months later, I noticed that he was at home. I got the feeling that something was going on which was above my head. He greeted me and went back into the kitchen, where he was cooking. I felt tense, and so went for a quick shower. I prayed under the shower that I might be able to cope with the situation, be able to support him. When I went back to the room, I felt as if I was walking on tip-toes. I went in and he pointed to a cutting lying on the table. He sat eating with his back to me. I read it and said, "That's new, a group like that." "Yes," he said, "I've joined it and I'm glad that we'll be able to meet there." "Great for you that such a group exists." I remained interested, for him. Just let him talk that evening. I felt that it was a relief to him, that talking to me did him good. I myself had the feeling that I was falling into an abyss. On the way home I cried: I had lost Adam as a life companion. I felt hopeless for days. Later I talked about it with my brother and he said: "You've had your eyes tight shut. What ordinary person allows a strange woman to have a shower in his house? You don't do that if you expect something more. I could have told you that he was a homosexual." So that was that.

I continued to go to Adam's house on Fridays. It struck me that he was usually at home. He let me read a letter that he had sent to his family and friends. He read the letter to me and for the first time I heard him utter the word homosexual. He went to association meetings and after a number of these said that he was going on vacation with a colleague. He was happy as a child but my spirits sagged for sorrow over my lost love. However, the feeling that we belonged together still remained. How would this situation develop?

Adam gradually had more contact with his friend. He came to visit me less and less. But we remained friends, and it was very nice when he came. He liked talking about his relationship and I continued to pay attention. He didn't dwell on what it meant for me. For him, little between us had changed.

When Adam and his friend went on vacation, I had to have another operation. My womb had to be removed. Adam came to visit me as soon as he returned. First of all he asked how I was. Then came the enthusiastic stories about the experiences with his friend. I tried to listen with interest, but at that moment I had a lot to cope with myself. I had lost my womb and the friend whom I so loved. After the splendid vacation I didn't think it impossible that I would lose him for ever.

After a few months problems developed between Adam and his friend. When the relationship broke down, Adam was very sad. I tried to comfort him. After several months he put in an advertisement. Looking for a new relationship. He asked whether he could use my address for correspondence. I agreed. I didn't think it very sensitive of him, but I didn't say anything. He wanted a firm relationship, but this wouldn't work. Once he embraced me and said, "I'm so happy with our friendship. Just sad that you aren't a boy." At that moment, on the one hand I felt offended, and on the other I wished that I were a boy. It was a painful situation, but I continued to love him.

In September 1981 Adam moved. I and another member of the parish helped him to move into his new house; it looked as though I was moving my own house. We went to buy carpets and curtains. During this period we had intimate physical contact. It happened quite unexpectedly. Later I felt upset and had guilt-feelings. What did I do? Surely making love with a priest was wrong? Was I indeed one of those "filthy women who help a priest to damnation"? Men couldn't help it: that was the way they were made. A woman had to be wiser, stronger. And so I bravely repeated all that I had been taught in my youth about men, women and their sexual characteristics. For a short moment.

In October we went to Paris together: to a hotel for the first time. I found this enormously exciting, and it was quite a special period in my life. I bought new clothes, and thought that a new time was dawning for me. For the first time I would be going out with a man, far from home. But I also felt anxious and thought: "As long as he doesn't murder me in Paris, to be rid of me. No one would think that he had done that." Just to be on the safe side, I told a friend, an older, wise woman, that we were going to Paris...

In Paris it was very ambiguous. It was great, but Adam got confused over his feelings. He found it nice to be with me, but he was also longing for a boy. Adam gave me a drawing of two naked figures, a man and a woman embracing. I had seen it and thought to myself, "O, if only I could do this with Adam, how happy I would be." When he bought it for me, he said, "I think that indicates what we feel for each other." It was a very intimate moment.

Later we looked at it together and sat there crying because it was such an ambiguous situation. On the way back we met Bishop Simonis in the train. We got hot and cross because this man seemed to have such an influence on our lives.

In June 1982 Adam told me what he felt for me and asked whether I was willing to go on through life with him. He had discovered that what he had constantly been looking for had always been there. I was over the moon and very confused. I was afraid that this might be a temporary situation and that I would have to get out of the way if the church told Adam I should. Or if a man should come into the picture. Adam behaved like someone in love. He always wanted to be with me. I found that splendid, but sometimes there were also difficulties. We couldn't always come out with our relationship. We resolved to go on vacation to a distant country. There we could enjoy each other without the eyes of the parish on us. We went off within ten days. We spent almost all of the first four weeks together in bed. We enjoyed each other's nearness and bodily contact. It was glorious!

Meanwhile I had moved, further from Adam's home but nearer to my work. The distance was a burden, but it also provided some freedom. My sister had problems and she and her daughter came to live with me. Adam suggested that I should temporarily live with him because my flat was too small for three people; we talked about whether I should go back to my own home when my sister had left. We didn't want circumstances to force us to live together. We wanted to decide in complete freedom what we wanted for our future. And that's what happened. After four months I returned to my flat.

Living so far from each other again took some getting used to. I kept visiting before he had to go to a meeting, or went to him when he got back. The result was that we went short on sleep. This began to wreak its toll. After much discussion we decided that I should live by myself so that Adam could get on with his work. I would look for a house for him in the neighbourhood. Then we could meet every day. We asked the pastors and the committee to look for a room for me. I had a tip that there was an empty flat in Adam's apartment block. To our joy it proved to be a flat in the same building but with an entrance through a different door. I bought it, and we began to alter it with the help of parishioners. During the alterations we decided to live together in my home. We would use Adam's home as his study. We put the telephone through so that he could be as available as possible to his parishioners. Adam came up with the suggestion of making an affidavit that if there were problems in work, in other words, if we were faced with a decision between his priestly work and me, the choice would be for our relationship. Psychologically this meant a lot to me. It gave me a form of protection and I would no longer be uncertain whether Adam would opt for me or the church. Otherwise our relationship is just as vulnerable as any other relationship.'

Finally I asked Eve how many people knew about her relationship. She said: 'Fortunately our relationship is known and indeed approved of by many parishioners and by our respective families. We know that we are accepted and welcome.'

The vow of celibacy and the formation of sexual relationships

'When we were discussing the conditional text on the vow of celibacy at seminary with the then bishop, I joined in the discussion rationally rather than with any feeling. The discussion as to

whether the vow of celibacy had any meaning or was meaningless was in full swing within the seminary walls. With many others I lived in expectation that the tradition of a celibate priesthood had had its long day and that it would rapidly be ended. I suspect that the bishop of the time had something of the same expectation in presenting us with a conditional vow of celibacy. We could make the oath on the following conditions:
– as long as the church requires the priest to live a celibate life.
– to the degree that one could foresee the consequences of the vow of celibacy.

When I made my vow of celibacy I thought that I would have no difficulty in remaining unmarried. I felt little need to form a relationship. At the same time I thought that there was no need to require priests to live a celibate life.

In retrospect I think that I didn't long for a relationship at that time because I had begun to note that my sexual orientation was of a homosexual kind. There was even a time when I found my vow of celibacy useful, because it was no longer important for me to discover whether I was homosexual, heterosexual or bisexual. But I did begin to oppose church statements which disapproved of or condemned the forming of homosexual relations. I took a stand in a discussion between younger men and the bishop, but this was not over my sexual preference. It was over church teaching on homosexuality. I also talked about it with Eve at a meeting on the issue in which we were both involved. Questions of my own sexual feelings were only really raised, and I only accepted them, when I read that an association of Catholic homosexual priests had been set up. For me this was a shock of recognition. I was not the only priest with a homosexual orientation. The association meant that there was a place where one could talk personally. I made Eve read the newspaper account about the setting up of the organization and told her that I wanted to make contact with it. At that moment I was so preoccupied with myself that I didn't for a moment ask myself what this information meant for Eve. I regarded her as a good friend with whom I could discuss such intimate things. Then everything happened in a rush. I had already begun to take the organization of my life into my own hands. I no longer lived in the clergy house but in a private apartment. Now I also had a desire to stop going through life alone. I needed a relationship. I thought that the association offered a safe way of finding such a relationship. I met someone there whom I found attractive and with whom I agreed to go on vacation. I took it for granted that this agreement was the beginning of a homosexual relationship. To begin with my partner accepted this. But after a couple of months he wanted to put an end to the relationship. In retrospect I think he was right. I've thought it all through. An agreement to go on vacation is not an agreement to have a sexual relationship, a loving relationship or a permanent friendship. The breaking off of the relationship woke me up, and I began to reflect on what I really wanted. I discovered that I wanted recognition of my homosexual orientation, both by myself and by others. I didn't want to go through life alone any longer, but wanted a permanent friendship. I recognized that I was interested in young men. I find them attractive to look at. I'm attracted by television programmes about sex generally and homosexuality in particular. At the same time I realized that such a permanent friendship was probably unattainable, because of the difference in age between me and a young man.

At the time when this was coming home to me, a woman friend made me think hard about my friendship with Eve. She asked me whether I realized what Eve felt for me and thought that I should come clean to Eve about the nature of our friendship. That made me reflect, and in a flash it became quite clear to me that I was longing for something which was already there: the marvellous permanent friendship which I sought was already there with Eve. I simply had to acknowledge it completely and say "yes". I didn't yet know whether I was capable of having a sexual relationship with Eve, but I began to become open to it. I was glad to discover that when I asked her, Eve wanted to go through life with me from then on. From that moment, for me the relationship with Eve was the permanent relationship that I was longing for. I found rest.

This doesn't mean that my sexual interest in young men has come to an end. It's still there, but no longer coupled with a longing for relations with a young man.

I haven't broken off my connection with the association of

homosexual pastors. However, I've changed it: I no longer go to the meetings but follow their publications, out of interest.

Since I have found my joy and rest in my loving relationship with Eve I have no further interest in what I should call my sexual interest: homosexual, heterosexual or bisexual. That doesn't matter. I'm no longer bothered about that kind of label.'

This story gives an important piece of the life of Eve and Adam, their way to each other, to their earthly paradise: sharing life with each other.

Eve and Adam live in a new form of partnership, a form of relationship which is not institutionalized, which may not exist and is denied by many. They are open because they want to show others that such a relationship is possible, that it has made them more complete people, bearers of God's image.

How did such a relationship come about? What do they themselves say about it?

How did you get to know each other and when was that?

He: 'We got to know each other in parish study groups in 1975. We were both thirty-three. It was a good contact that later grew into a friendship. This was also possible because our circumstances changed. I went to live by myself, and so did Eve.

The first thing that we had in common was our religious interest in the liturgy. Eve was finding a new orientation in her life. She moved house around this time. I found it natural to help her with the little jobs that such a move involves, when you do it without friends. By chance we lived near to each other. Of course, that also led to close contact. I found it quite natural for her to use my shower, since she had none in her new home. Our friendship deepened through ordinary practical things.'

She: 'From the beginning I noticed that we had a lot in common. Interest in religious questions, in dance, music, the theatre. We understood one another. He seemed to be my other half. I noticed that I was often looking for reasons to make contact with him. At the beginning of our friendship I was a religious. At this time I didn't accept any sexual feelings in myself. They were a sin. I entrusted myself to him as a kind of extra. He added a dimension to my life. I felt rich: I was no longer alone.

After a few years I moved out of my religious group to an

apartment. I wanted to decide for myself how I should live. The social pressure had become too great for me. I wanted to rediscover my lost self, away from the group. My family helped me move, and so did Adam. He came to visit me. This was the first time in my life that I had someone special. I was amazed. After a talk about the move he suggested that he might do some jobs. I still remember his remark: "Just right, eh, father doing some jobs and mother in the kitchen!" It was as though he aroused something in me. It confused me. Adam stayed that evening and I found it great to be together like that.

We met regularly through our activities in the parish. We also saw each other outside, for example at the anniversaries of members of the group. I thought that splendid. But there was something else. I was a member of my religious community. I lived alone and kept feeling a longing for a companion in life. I felt that I was being torn apart: contact with the community decreased; I seemed to be growing away from it, and that provoked tensions in me. After eighteen years of religious life in a congregation, I resolved to quit. I told Adam my decision. We talked about it for a long time. About that process in me, not about my feelings for him. I didn't want that. He was (and still is) a functioning priest. I didn't want to endanger his priestly life and didn't know what he felt for me. After I had obtained the official annulment of my vows, I had a remarkably ambiguous feeling. A feeling of liberation from restrictive bonds and social control. And a feeling of being a stranger in a society which wasn't really mine. For me Adam was a fixed point I could fall back on. He thought the friendship with me very splendid, but also said that he was a priest and that I couldn't expect more of the friendship. I replied that I didn't expect more.'

At an early stage did you discuss belief, the church, and church regulations?

He: 'The friendship was good and at that point church regulations weren't in question. To begin with, other factors played a role: discussions with Bishop Simonis about homosexuality. To this degree there was a conflict with the bishop. Eve and I were involved in it because we were active in the liturgy. I could talk to Eve about it: that was very important for me and gave content to our friendship.

At a later stage, when our friendship became more intimate, I had no guilt feelings about my vow. For me, the vow to the church or to God was always conditional. We had discussed it with the bishop at the seminary and agreed that we could make a conditional vow of celibacy. However, this formulation was allowed only once. The next year a subsequent group of ordinands had to use the classical formula again. For our group the formulation of the conditional vow of celibacy was never revoked. I had no problems with it, and felt no guilt. There was no reason to. I didn't feel bound to the vow.'

Eve, what did you feel for this man?

She: 'I never thought, this man or no one. He was a priest, so it could never go further than friendship. That is very valuable in itself. Deep in my heart I had the conviction that we belonged together. That was quite special; I also felt something like, "I won't allow anyone to take this feeling, this conviction, from me. What is intrinsically good is good."

It wasn't so important to ask whether our contact would ever become a firm relationship. It was good as it was at that moment.'

Can you tell us about the first time that you had intimate contact, that you became 'man and wife'?

He: 'Becoming "man and wife" for the first time was a tense occasion for me. I didn't know whether I could do it or not. It didn't work very well. It seemed more a confirmation of my homosexual feelings.'

She: 'I felt tense, because of his homosexual feelings and the anxiety that he was perhaps doing this for me. So it was an ambiguous feeling, on the one hand something natural, on the other an anxious trial.'

What is now so attractive for you in your relationship?

She: 'The attractive thing for me is that we're such good friends.'

He: 'That we feel at home with one another. That's why we can live together so well.'

They both have the feeling that their relationship will continue like this. They see a sunny future ahead. I asked them whether they also had any advice for other couples in such a situation.

'Every situation is different. But there's something important which applies to everyone: be honest about your feelings.'

They had always been like this. It had not always been easy, but for them it was the only way. The church will remain, they think, and they have a role in it, they make a contribution. They don't feel pioneers. They also know that there are many others who have a relationship. They want to pass on to others what they have learned with and through each other.

'You learn to reflect and talk about the form you give such a relationship. It isn't intrinsically necessary to give up priestly work. You can give one another the certainty that the relationship is number one. We've had that put down in an affidavit.'

Eve above all was very clear when I asked her for advice for those in similar positions.

'Make agreements with your partner and put them down in a fixed form, so that there is an equal situation. When nothing has been set down, the priest's ministry contines to dominate the relationship.'

How do you feel, Adam, about living quite differently from what the institutional church expects of you?

He: 'It isn't nice. I would rather live differently. But it's important to live honestly. We can't come out openly with our feelings for each other without consequences for the exercising of my priestly tasks. Otherwise we live like any other couple.'

Ordinary people. They live together. They both have their work and are devoted to it. They are valued in their neighbourhood. Eve and Adam. It would be a pity if the church had to lose them.

I want openness!

Surely few women have a relationship with a priest? Surely they are an exception? Perhaps some rather unstable women have a short-term relationship with a priest? Ank didn't agree.

'When I read the article in *Hervormd Nederland* I had the sense of being taken back ten years. Many memories came to the surface.' She got to know Arend in a period in which much was possible. Arend was a fiery champion of radicalism. He was fond of talking to people, including married couples. Sometimes more than just friendship developed. Above all, Ank didn't want to feel cramped at the beginning of their relationship. 'For me, relations with Arend were strange and unclear. I asked questions. At that time they were about professional visits, perhaps a visit to a woman who couldn't talk to her husband.' She noticed that other priests also had such unclear forms of friendship. Within her relationship she couldn't put up with that any longer and wanted either to break it off or get some clarity. 'Why did I opt for the latter? In the first place I loved Arend; he was attractive and we had many interests in common. So there was something to fight for. I also had a kind of inner compulsion to sort out this inauthentic situation.' She described how unsettled Arend was at this time, probably because he had to hide a lot from her. There were three women who were getting 'special' attention from him. The situations were virtually the same. Young families who didn't know of each other's existence and in which the husband was the occasion for a friendship. Sometimes he was involved in work in the parish. Later this man became the excuse for the relationship which arose. To those around, the women seemed chaste mothers and partners in a good Catholic family, where the priest visited the house as a good friend. All those involved found it difficult to put an end to these relationships, but it happened, since Ank fought for her relationship. She was a different woman from Arend's other women friends. She was free, she needed no help or guidance. She made demands on a relationship.

'That was often difficult, but I can also see the advantages. I have the feeling that through these problems we built up a quite unique relationship.' At this time she was never able to talk with anyone about her relationship and the problems that were beginning. After that, things got better. She resolved to come and live at the clergy house. She even went so far as to tell the parish quite boldly. Almost everyone reacted positively; only a few didn't – precisely those who had influence within the hierarchy. The reaction of the local church leaders was that as long as it didn't develop into a great scandal, as long as they didn't openly flaunt their relationship, they had to go their own way. But they said that this mustn't be a precedent. Ank really wanted that: establishing limits, looking for new forms. Only that wasn't possible; they had to continue to keep quiet. They had one problem less because they could live quietly together. So peace and quiet were restored in the diocese and that is still the case.

Over the years they have built up a good relationship in which they are both happy. Now and then problems arise which are connected with the fact that he is a priest, that they can't appear in public as partners in the ordinary way. 'A short time ago we were at a party. Other priests with their women friends were also there. What did I see? The women sat primly in their own circle. The priests sat talking to one another far from their own partners. Even there they had to be like that for everyone.' On that occasion she wanted it to be shown that she belonged with her partner, as other couples do. That didn't happen with them. She remarked that it is important for the priest that his partner can look after herself. Feminist women sometimes? 'There's something in that,' she felt. 'At the beginning I too thought, "I must look after myself, since he has too many duties." Sometimes that was neatly connected with self-interest. Sometimes it was also compulsive resistance to the need for ties.' What Ank has learned from this situation is that openness is important, that you must work for it and maintain it. Her partner would prefer not to be reminded of that time. She couldn't talk about it then. Now she does have the chance and thinks it important that other women should learn something from her situation. 'Our relationship is great, and that can only come about by being open to outsiders.'

Her partner has also learned from her. He has become more open, and that deserves respect. Certainly if you've come a long way. He sees their relationship as something he doesn't want to get out of. His life has become richer as a result.

He had enough

They first got to know each other in church, then at work. He was still young, in his middle thirties. She was a couple of years younger than him. They were just friends for ten years, they were fond of each other.

Ten years is a long time: you get to know each other well and intimacy grows. He asked her to come and live with him in the clergy house, simply because it was good to have a housekeeper with whom you got on well. That lasted four years. To begin with all went well. Really everything happened naturally: a deeper relationship developed, friendship became love which was also expressed physically. In the time before, too, in the period when there was just friendship between them, a bond had developed. They both knew about celibacy, and you don't break that vow. But after such a long time you clearly know how you feel about each other. Then it makes no sense to call love anything else because only friendship is allowed between a priest and a woman.

So she lived in the clergy house as a housekeeper. That looked better, a pastor who needs a housekeeper.

He was a sensitive person. What attracted her so much about him was that she could talk to him so easily. He was attractive, loving and attentive. She was a warm woman. She had many dealings with people in her work, knew precisely what people who had a call on her did, what they needed. She was passionate and independent. A good hostess, she could cook well and gave him a home.

No one knew of their relationship. They enjoyed their happiness in the quiet seclusion of the clergy house and became richer as a result. He was a better pastor, she was a better nurse. And no one said anything special about it. Certainly both of them were aware that he was no longer keeping his vow to live a celibate life. But they also felt that their life was a service to their neighbours, and that was something else that had been promised. And no one was suffering harm from their lives; quite the contrary. They found joy in their love and sex until the moment when she noticed that the approach was increasingly coming from her. Was something wrong? Was there perhaps someone else? Earlier he had been an attentive man who often touched her and also sought physical contact with her. One day he suddenly announced that he no longer wanted to have intercourse with her. What would you feel as a woman then?

Thousands of questions without an answer.

'For years he concealed from me that he had someone else. But I knew that she often came to him and that they went on vacation together. We couldn't talk about it.'

That broke her up, and caused many problems.

The relationship ended, it no longer worked. She had had enough of the little lies, the fibs, the half-truths. There was a time when she pushed away the thought that there was another woman in his life. 'There were also good periods. But later they got fewer.' Did they talk about their faith? 'Not much. In retrospect, our conversations were only superficial.' But she was imprisoned with all her questions and her pain. Now life goes on; five years have passed since then. For a short time she was happy. There was a period when she was a housekeeper in the clergy house and worked as a nurse. When this combination became too much, she gave up her outside career. Later came the move and the search for a new job. A high price for short-lived happiness. She had wanted it to turn out differently. She is really still uncommunicative about it. Says that it's a liberation for her and that she can now talk about it with someone. But she still doesn't know how to express the break in her life.

'Priests must remember that they can break a person. Happily I can now be somewhat detached, but something has happened that has changed my life and the pain is there, even if it's growing less.'

Know my smile

Know my smile
if you can
my light from within
to take myself
where I not yet am

Know my word
that you hear
in deepest silence
directed from you
to where I do not know myself

Know my wish
God and man
my wide longing
to embrace everything
I want to reach for

Know my strength
which works
in vessels of my actions
streamladen
by your trust in life

Know my all
that shall become
pure receiving
is not yet born
being waits for you

Karel Douven

One of the many

In May 1975 my husband suddenly died. I was forty, and was left with a boy of twelve and a Down's Syndrome daughter of fourteen. At the time three priests were living in the clergy-house in our parish. We had good contacts with one of them as a family and my husband had a special contact with one of the others. He really wasn't a parish priest but a weekend pastor: he also gave lectures and wrote books. My husband could talk easily with him and gradually a friendship developed, though they really didn't visit each other's homes.

About six months after my husband died, this pastor – I shall call him Paul – made contact with me. He was preparing a radio broadcast about women who found themselves alone. He asked whether he could have a talk with me, which he did. He was (and still is) a captivating man. I thought that when I was still married, but at the time I never had any special feelings: he was just a charming man. During our conversation about the radio broadcast I spoke very openly with him and entrusted him with a number of poems which I had written in my period of despair. Poems about my feelings of loneliness, insecurity, now having to sleep alone with no one next to me. When he left, he kissed me passionately. I found that difficult. I felt wretched and alone, but that wasn't what I was looking for.

It didn't stop at that one visit. He became a regular visitor and slowly I found that I was looking forward to his visits. I told him so. I also said that I didn't want our friendship, which is what you could call it, to cause problems for him. He said that it didn't.

It overwhelmed me when he suggested that we should go to bed together. I had never thought of this for a moment, because to me he was a priest. The fact that we could talk together well, be quiet together or play a game was enough for me. But we did go to bed together a few months later and I honestly have to say that it gave our friendship an extra dimension. I blossomed again, and light came back to my eyes, I got more energy, and life smiled on me again. People told me that I looked better. It didn't bother me that I couldn't talk to anyone. I thought it a pity, but I also understood that things had to remain anonymous. I had a precious secret and didn't find it difficult to go visiting alone or to go on holiday with the children alone. It wouldn't have been easy for him to be on holiday with the children: he wasn't used to it. So I always had an explanation why certain things were impossible. Now I realize only too well how naive I was. I saw things once too often through rose-coloured spectacles. Even in church we didn't acknowledge each other: we acted as if we were strangers even if we had spent the previous night together. No one had even a suspicion.

That lasted for a number of years. And I didn't get any happier. I found that when it suited him he hid behind his priesthood. That he didn't always take advantage of the opportunities that there were.

When the guardian of my children died I asked him whether he would take over the guardianship. He reacted in an almost hostile way. I knew that it wasn't impossible for priests to take over a guardianship. But for him something of this kind was just not on. I looked for another solution, swallowed the unpleasantness, but didn't want to lose him.

Until a particular moment when I was in a group where there was talk of Paul. Someone spoke of his relationship with a woman with whom he had been on vacation. My world collapsed. I made a terrible scene and told him what a bastard he was. It proved that he "lodged" with this woman two nights a week and they were the very days on which, as I realized in retrospect, he never came to me: Tuesday and Saturday.

I felt terribly left in the lurch, all the more so since Paul couldn't cope with the situation and disappeared. I couldn't keep this to myself and took our parish priest into my confidence. It proved that Paul had relations with many more women. I had the feeling of being back in a process of mourning, but a different kind of process, much more cruel, much more painful, because I didn't "want" to mourn. Did no one know? After a time he tried to restore something of the relationship; he felt that we still had much good in common and said that at the moments when he was with me he was "only for me" and told yet more nice tales, enough to make you cry. I had a great deal of difficulty, though when I said this he swept it away. He thought I wasn't on his level, that I wanted exclusiveness, and that was cramping. But when I thought that the next day he would be in bed with another woman I found that intolerable.

I asked myself what our relationship had meant to him. Clearly it had been quite different for me, not what it was for him. Even when he was at home with me he had never told me that he had another woman or several women.

Our relationship settled down on something of a Platonic basis, but I had the idea that it didn't mean very much to him. It wasn't very nice for me to feel that the next day or the day after he would be with someone else who was more pleasing to him. So I couldn't go on and then broke with him completely. I felt too good to be one in a series of many.

However, a difficult point remained: he still lived at the clergy house and meanwhile had become more involved in the parish. In the course of time I had taken on certain tasks within the parish, some of which I now dropped because I couldn't bear to encounter him. But the more you cast such things off, the more isolated you become. You can't explain to anyone else why you're dropping them. I got asked direct questions if I made even the slightest negative remarks about Paul. Here everyone was on his side. Moreover he kept on making yet other relations. I tracked down a women with whom he has such a relationship. Like me she was left alone after her marriage and is content with a little satisfaction even though it causes her suffering. Moreover rivalry has developed between her and another "friend"', so that it's almost impossible for her to to bear the thought of someone else. I try to help her a bit and convince her that it can't be the purpose of any relationship that you hurt yourself so much. Then you get a block and there's no room for growth. I've already thought of moving, but on the other hand I refuse to sacrifice my nice home and my dear friends. I've now taken some people into my confidence, but the confrontation remains difficult. I'm now trying to distance myself fairly unobtrusively from parish activities and to become active in other areas. That's something, and I now feel stronger. I'm trying to hold on to the good that there was, though the sorrow of this situation will remain woven into my life. It makes me insecure that he branded me as obsessive, because I didn't want to be one of his many women. I was dealing with the situation wrongly, he said, because I couldn't attain his level. On the other hand I know that many people think me worthwhile. I hold firm to that and that gives me trust in the future.

At first I doubted whether I wanted to tell my story. But when I read Cardinal Simonis's reaction to the report about women friends of priests, namely that such a thing didn't happen, I didn't hesitate for a moment.

It's not so much a matter of whether or not priests want a woman friend, but rather that these women can be broken, and that's sad.

I refuse to call myself a victim, though in essence that's what I am.

As long as there is silence or it is denied that priests have relationships with women and that as well as the good relations there are many in which tears are shed, nothing can be done, and there is nowhere to turn to in your sorrow.

I don't want priests to be punished or dismissed from office, since they are usually people with first-class qualities, but by recognizing and identifying abuses some guidance can perhaps be given so that priests, too, learn how to behave in a relationship. That could spare women (and perhaps also priests) much sorrow.

Education and training repress and silence many feelings, but that doesn't mean that they're "really" dead. Happily, I can say on the one hand, but on the other these feelings must be guided into good channels, so that joy and growth can be experienced even in a relationship with a priest.'

Mortal sin

'I wrote to the bishop,' she said, 'after a television broadcast in which he was interviewed. In it he denied knowing any priests who had a relationship with a woman.' Hedwig wrote to him that she at any rate had a relationship with a priest. 'He wrote back that I must stop it immediately and go to confession, since I was living in mortal sin.' She also asked the Catholic Broadcasting Corporation why this subject was never discussed. 'I got the impression from the clergy adviser that they daren't expose this issue publicly.' She herself is very free about it, and her children, family and acquaintances know. And they accept it. 'But Ben doesn't dare to come out with it. That's often led to problems in our relationship. I've put an end to it five times over all these years. But we always keep looking each other up again.'

With some interruptions, Hedwig has had a relationship with a priest for thirteen years. They got to know each other through an advertisement which she placed for a travelling companion. 'He replied, and didn't say in the first instance that he was a priest. He told me that he was a teacher, and he did in fact give lessons in a middle school. He was forty-five and I was thirty-five. Before we went on vacation together I had discovered that he was a priest as well as a teacher.' She had told him that she didn't want any sexual contact, but just a travelling companion, and he agreed. 'I thought that you ran less risk with a priest than with another man.' But things turned out differently, much more complicated.

Long and vigorous conversations followed. 'He thought me prudish and said that I knew nothing about the faith: God had created man and women. Priests might not marry because they had to be available for the church, but that didn't mean that they couldn't have any relationships. He did suggest that we should live together but not marry, because he wanted to remain a priest.'

She began to fall in love with him. In the end she was a free woman and she thought that he himself had to answer for what he did. And so it came about, falling in love, petting and sex. 'In the sexual sphere he was very inventive, constantly did different things, and was very patient and tender.'

They promised to remain faithful to each other for life. He was attractive to her because of his cheerfulness, his patience and his enterprising nature. 'He was also very well educated, and that spoke to me.' In the first years of their relationship and even now sometimes, he made her think of an adolescent. 'He was always reading modern books full of sex and violence. He also seemed like an adolescent in another respect; he took things apart at home and could never put them together again. Then he left me with the pieces. He wanted to do all kinds of things, even irresponsible things. He always went to bed late and got up around noon, had much bluff and bravura, but when it came to the point he was so very sad and I had to go to his help. He also went to the cinema often and loved the good life.'

Earlier they would talk a lot about the faith, but they always got into rows over it. 'He asserted things which were just not true, and so we avoid that kind of thing now. Among other things he says that the church never said that people had to have large families. That they wanted these themselves! I myself brought up seven. I know just how hard it was. He also says that the church would already have admitted women to the priesthood long ago if women had wanted that themselves. But he claimed that they didn't.' She had asked him whether they would be able to live together later, when he was sixty-five. And Ben said, 'I don't know yet. They're going to build an old people's home at our club, and perhaps I'll go straight there. Moreover it will depend on which of the two of us is best suited.' She then got terribly cross. He said that she didn't understand. 'We grew up together as brothers, and I can't leave them (!) in the lurch.' Indeed he doesn't leave them in the lurch even now: sometimes he goes on holiday with a colleague. Nor does he visit her so often; he's afraid that it will all get out and he will lose his job. She looks round carefully when she goes to see him. 'He has always insisted that the priesthood and his colleagues came first; I only come after that. And then I still have to make a good reconnaisance.'

The last two years he has no longer taken the initiative in making love. 'I asked him what the reason for this was, and he said, "It must come from you." When I said that that certainly didn't used to be the case, he didn't reply. I suppose that now he's wise to himself, that as long as I take the initiative he's doing it for me.'

Earlier they saw each other very little. 'Often three months would go by and then he was there only for a couple of days. He could cope better than I. Sometimes I felt like a cheap prostitute, from whom he could also get free food and drink. In recent months he's come more often. I moved not so long ago and he helped me with some jobs. I much appreciated that. Over the years he's got more skilful and likes that sort of thing.' He's a sensitive man but can't express himself well; however, that's slowly getting better. She's just an attractive and passionate woman with whom he finds homeliness and warmth.

A long time ago she had left the Catholic church. She can still remember the hypocrisy of her pastor. Her husband left her. The pastor then said that she couldn't get a divorce. 'If you do, you give your husband an opportunity to marry again, and that's wrong. Marriage is till death you do part. If you had no children (but she had seven), we could argue that the marriage had never been consummated, that no sexual act had taken place, but now that's no longer possible.' She also recognized some church hypocrisy in Ben. He also concedes this: 'In my training I learned to creep through the meshes of the net.' And he does so, loves everyone, the congregation and his woman friend. Over the years Hedwig has learned to be somewhat detached, looser, and above all not to expect too much. 'It's not the sex that's important for us but knowing that there is someone who cares for you, who listens to you and waits for you, the homeliness, the warmth. Someone who fills in for you if in one way or another you fall short.'

Mary gets pregnant and has a daughter

Mary was fifteen when she went to France as an au pair. There she got to know a Dutch priest of thirty-five. She could live with him. In that small French village no one thought it strange that the priest had a girl in the house. Mary was still young and had had hardly any sexual education from her parents. Priest John gave it to her: vivid instruction. A relationship developed. He was attracted by her and she also found him attractive: 'I thought it great to be able to do something in return for all that he did for me.' No one knew anything of their relationship. John also had other relationships during and before his relations with Mary. 'A young woman even committed suicide,' Mary relates. She continued to live with John from her fifteenth to her eighteenth year. Then she went to the Netherlands to take up training. Until she was twenty-seven they met a few times a year in France or the Netherlands. Then there was sexual contact.

One day she found that she was pregnant. Priest John insisted on an abortion. She didn't want that. He proposed adoption. But Mary also refused that and resolved to bring up the child herself. 'Psychologically he couldn't bear a child of his running around.' Mary worked nights and by day looked after her daughter. Some years later she met the man she was to marry. She told him about her daughter and the relationship from which she was born. 'I also wanted a father for my daughter'. She was twenty-seven when she got married and has another four children by her marriage.

She has good memories of her experience of sex with John. So had John, but he had difficulty with the fact that he had broken his vow of chastity.

In subsequent years Mary went regularly to France with her husband and children to meet the priest. 'We had no more sexual contact after my marriage. But I did massage him and kiss him,' she said. Mary and John's daughter is now married. Sometimes she visits her father. They have a friendly contact. Mary asks herself what it is like for John to see his daughter now and then. It caused her great pain that John was left alone when she married. Her husband didn't understand this. He thought that the bond had been broken. 'I can't share with anyone the sorrow and the pain which of course are still with me.' She also discussed the faith a lot with John. She is still a practising Catholic. 'He was and is a good spiritual director. He formed me socially, raised my prayer life to a higher level and introduced me to meditation.'

In the period when she had contact with John they went to make their confession together in another diocese. Then her relationship was also discussed and she was asked whether it wouldn't be better if they parted. 'But this was not made a condition of our absolution. I also think that that was because we both had good experiences and didn't live at each other's expense.'

What characteristics did John value most in Mary? To this she replied: 'My honesty, my childlike openness. My complete availability and care.' She found this care important in their dealings together. She also has a message for the church representatives: 'Don't criticize, there's already enough of that, and there's no need for it. Just think: "I was lonely and you comforted me, I longed for someone, for some warmth, for love, and you gave it me." Don't be afraid as a representative of the church to put an arm round a woman and say, "Thank you for being there when I needed you. Thank you for having the courage to come back when that was asked of you. Know that I shall always be there to listen to your story, to share your sorrow with you." '

She remains loyal to her church, but also asks for understanding and compassion. She knows a bit of what goes on in the church. Finally she remarked, 'After a confession a priest embraced and kissed me. I felt that this wasn't the first and only time that he had done this.'

She doesn't think it bad for priests to have relationships, but she does feel that they are often all too free with women's feelings. 'I think we both have good memories of our relationship.' Memories which have become flesh in the form of their child.

I want to get my story off my chest

'I want to get my story off my chest,' she said, 'but really you never get rid of this bit of history from your life.' She was forty-four when she told me her story in which the priest plays such a dramatic role. She is married and has four children. For some time she has again been under the care of a psychiatrist. She has made her mark in art: she models splendid things. Later she told how she could live as it were a second life in the world of her art. How in this way she could shut out her other life. That was her way of survival.

'It began when I was seven. He was rector of the convent school I went to.'

Her parents had five children and she was the youngest. The rector of the school was a family friend. He came along regularly and sometimes baby-sat in the evenings when the parents went out. Then he would put the two youngest to bed, her older brother and her. They would first play a little and romp with each other. That was nice. He knew Christine well and it was also very nice that he walked a little way with her when she was going to school. Or she went with him when he had been visiting her parents. 'Go a little way with Herman,' her mother would say. And full of trust she would put her little hand in the big hand of the man who wore such an immaculate black suit. He also once went with the whole family on vacation. Then Christine and her brother would wake him up in the morning and play with him. That went on for about a year.

Once when he was putting her to bed in the evening, her parents were on a visit somewhere, he suddenly put his hand in her knickers. She didn't understand. Now, years afterwards, she recalls how it began very slowly: a first touch, a gentle hand, a fatherly cuddle.

Afterwards, when she went past his house on the way to school, the man in black was standing there and waved to her to come in. He was nice to her, but again there was also a touch on her skin where no one had ever touched her. He seemed to find this nice. She didn't understand. He was always going to her parents and everyone though that nice. He had even helped her father find a better job. And he was always very friendly to mother and the children.

Once a number of girls at school laughingly told one another what they did with their friends. At that time she must have been eleven or twelve. One girl told how she had dared to give a boy a kiss in a quiet alley. Another girl told how she had got a ring from her boy friend. Christine had no boy friend, but she wanted to say something about her friend, the attractive man who often went walking with her. She didn't want to fall short of the other girls and told them how this rector, yes, the rector of the school, once put his hand in her knickers. One of the girls seems to have passed the story on, since a few days later the head of the school brought her out of the gym lesson for a confidential talk. In the office. Was what she had told these girls true?

'Yes,' said Christine. The head, a nun, thought that her parents should know this. Her parents heard the story and told the rector about it. He promised that he wouldn't do it again. 'But when I got home everyone kept quiet about the fact that there had been a conversation about it, my parents and he, when I had expected that they would be cross with me.'

Next time she went along the way to school he was again standing there, this man in black. He gestured to her to come in. 'Do you know that you could get me in prison by telling such things? Would you want that?' No, she didn't, what would other people think of her? He was always so nice to everyone. And surely her parents were very keen on him? 'Promise that you will never talk to anyone about it again.' So she kept quiet and tried to remain nice to everyone, including him.

It wasn't easy; often she loathed him. Sometimes she was also deliberately unpleasant, but nothing helped. He continued to go his way.

And so it went on for years. Even in middle school. Sometimes he would come to her house and wait until her parents had gone out. He would look after the little ones. Sometimes it happened at his house. The parents regularly let the two youngest children have a few days holiday with their family friend. When her brother had gone to sleep he had free play. There was constant stroking, his hands went everywhere, he desired her body. Not violently, gently, but compellingly. And constantly there was the feeling of the cocoon in which she was trapped: you couldn't get out, you had to keep quiet, you didn't want to make him unhappy and your resistance was broken when you saw that he enjoyed touching your body. But you didn't understand. What you did understand was that you had to keep quiet, since it was something that wasn't good. 'Would you want to get me into prison?' When it was over you were relieved. If you could go to school without the man in black standing at the window you were happy. And if he was standing there, you couldn't do anything but go in. He gestured you to come. You endured his power, you simply couldn't do anything against it, like someone when emotions are too much to take.

She remembers how it was at the clergy house to which he had moved in the meantime. 'Clergy houses are cold, uncanny and spooky in one way or another. I was always expecting the creak of a stair or the squeak of a door. Sometimes I woke up with his hand in my knickers. Sometimes I kept asleep in the hope that he would then go away again, as sometimes also happened. At other times I was awake and saw him standing by my bed in his underwear. Before he crept into bed with me he first made the sign of the cross.'

That was one side of the man in black: his naked upper half and the lower half of his body covered by underwear. The other side was the nice uncle who gave Christine nice presents, took her to the ballet, bought books for her and a transistor radio. Sometimes she could choose nice clothes from his brother who made garments for a big business. He introduced her to the world of culture and literature. But also to the world of solitude, lack of feeling, hatred of being touched. There also remained the question why someone should do such a thing, what drove them to it. And why make the sign of the cross? Did that sometimes bring the two worlds together? Bind them?

'At all events, no one held anything against him, no one denied him holidays and hotel rooms. Later there were those evenings when he had to be in A or in B for a lecture, and then he would promise me a play which was on there, or a ballet or a good film that I was crazy about. He would talk of staying in a hotel, always two rooms, only one of which was used.'

Did her parents think that he had changed his behaviour? She doesn't know, and perhaps that will never be clear.

When Christine was eighteen her menstruation stopped. Pills, powders and drinks didn't help. She became anorexic and ate a minimum. 'To hospital,' said the gynaecologist, 'for investigation.' When the rector came to see her she got a separate room. That was quieter than the big ward with all those other people. The investigation showed nothing; there was no physical sign. The gynaecologist asked whether she had had a shock, a car suddenly braking behind her or something of the kind. She denied this, but it made her think. She told the rector what the gynaecologist had asked her. The rector had meanwhile become a pastor. She also told him that she thought that he and 'the secret' were the reason for her sickness. The rector then asked a gynaecologist friend whether it was possible that sexual abuse could lead to an interruption of menstruation. There was such a person in his parish . . .

Finally he telephoned her gynaecologist. She immediately said, 'That's it.'

The silence was broken. Now she could talk.

He took her away from school. Arranged a free afternoon for her. He spoke about himself: 'As a boy of twelve I was asked whether I wanted to marry or become a priest.' He opted for the first, but people (why, he didn't say) found him more suited for the second. 'That was the explanation he gave.'

With the help of a friend she succeeded in changing her life. Rows at home; she went away. She tried to regain power over her body. Her body was never really her own. Constantly there was the man in black who demanded it, who wanted to play with it for his own pleasure. For her at first there was only the anxiety that someone might come. Later there was the bond of a shared secret in which the small amount of friendliness and attention that he gave her was enough to make her submit to everything else. Between her eighth and eighteenth year. He had always planned to be able to bless her marriage. Hoped that one day she would get married and he could go on. But that never happened.

She married the friend of her youth and together they had four children. But there was always the thought of the man in black who had also been in love with her. The children's friend who at the same time had destroyed her childlike feelings.

There were difficult periods in her marriage, months of great depression. It got a bit better when her first son was born. Then she saw how defenceless and small the mark of a man can also be. How much care this little male needed.

'After it all I met him twice more. I wanted to round it off one way or another.' The first time he came to her home. She was already married by then. They talked of this and that, as often happens in situations when people are confused. 'For me it was like sitting in judgment. He himself asked, "Do you still remember that one time I was such a nuisance?" But I didn't know what he meant... He had reduced all those nine years to "that one time". I couldn't reply.'

He also told her how he had been under the care of a psychiatrist for years. 'I couldn't respond to that either. Had it been any use? Should I burden him with more than was necessary?'

At an early age she had escaped into her art, where she built her own world, alongside this other world in which she had to shut off her emotions. She experienced her emotions in her art. She was successful there. She told me that in the hotel where she once met him there is now a statue that she made. As if she was prompted to bind these two worlds together, to bring them into synthesis. And she's trying that. For years she was intermittently in therapy. Recently she's begun again. She wants to be able to go down the street where he once got her into a doorway and felt in her knickers. To be able to go through the village without being pursued by forsakenness and solitude for weeks. She wants to try to remove the traces of the man in black because he still haunts her life after all these years.

Looking back on a relationship

Jos filled in the questionnaire which I used for my investigation. When we met she already had many questions and still felt pain about the way in which everything had happened. She also joined in the meetings. By writing some things down and thinking and talking about them, she is a good deal clearer. For her the relationship is now finished and assimilated. This is what she writes about her understanding of it.

'It is now five and a half years since U, I shall just call him U, went off to Africa. At the time I didn't in fact feel that our relationship was over. I can't say precisely when I did begin to feel this.

How did I come to begin anything with U? "Who led whom astray?" What did our relationship mean?

I had already known him for some years. When I still didn't know him very well I went on holiday with a group. He was also one of this group. Shortly before the holiday I had been raped in my home by a strange man; I didn't know whether I had got over it sufficiently. I had to take someone into my confidence and chose him. He helped me several times during the holiday by giving me a listening ear and putting an arm round me.

That same vacation I got to know my first girl friend. He seemed to accept my lesbianism and understood my struggle against injustices towards homosexuals and lesbians, gays and dikes. Sometimes he had difficulties with my fierceness.

Our relationship began when U came to work in the same city. The relationship with my girl friend had gone wrong. It was now three years later.

He "led me astray". He asked me for the first kiss. After that we constantly went on step by step over the course of two months. He was cautious and scrupulously asked now and then whether he was going too far. He was also a man: he knew my history, knew that I had been raped. I felt respected and drawn to him as a person. I also approved of his cheerfulness, his political attitudes, his courage also to stick his own neck out in a conservative world like the Catholic church. And then he was the first man I had met who didn't want to penetrate my body immediately he made a sexual approach. He allowed me room to give form to my sexuality at my own pace. That was something new for me.

Our sex had a distinctive form. There was no sexual intercourse, though once it almost got that far. He was afraid when he discovered that I didn't use contraceptives. Our sex consisted of all kinds of touching, stroking, which clearly went beyond the character of a cuddle. At least that is my view, when you caress each other's body: penis, breasts and vagina.

Why do I write this now? The moment I came into contact with Tineke, who wanted to write a dissertation on the (ex-)women of priests, it increasingly became clear to me that I wanted to break through a tabu. To be just as radical as I was accustomed to be over my being a lesbian.

I had told people in "my circle" that I had a relationship with U, was in love with him and that he knew this. But my circle of friends and acquaintances, men and women, partially overlapped with his. And subsequently I saw that I had begun to avoid precisely this set of my friends and acquaintances. That to protect him there I had begun to keep my mouth shut. That was never agreed, but from his reactions when we were petting in his house and he heard people coming up the stairs, it was clear that he "didn't want to get trapped". Only afterwards did I see that I had fitted in with this at a particular time. I didn't want to go along with that any longer. I wanted to break the silence.

Some years beforehand I had left the church, and now openly identified myself with the radical 8 May movement... No one asked me at the time why I was there. But if I see them again and they ask me, I know what I shall tell them.

Not to damage him, but because I want to be honest and open about my life. If he hadn't wanted that, he should have thought of what he was starting. He knew me well enough to know that I talked openly with people, even knew my sexual life-style. I never promised him not to talk about it with certain people. I can't force him to do that, but he can't force me to be silent either. And with this decision I've broken the chains in which I had imprisoned myself by "sacrificing" myself for his future. When I told him about this in a letter, I got a quick reaction from him. For years I had put questions to him in countless letters and had to wait months for a reply. His replies didn't answer my questions. And now suddenly there was a very clear reaction; according to him we just had a good friendship, no relationship. For "we didn't have intercourse, not in the sense of sexual intercourse or living together..." And over the last years our link was only by letter.

This reaction from him closed the door for me. Someone who when pushed into a corner denies a whole piece of sexual experience is finished as far as I am concerned. He knew very well that I was in love and saw our behaviour as a relationship. He never called his feeling being in love, but he never denied that we had a relationship. He did, though, make it clear to me that he wanted to remain a priest and never wanted to marry or let the relationship develop. But that also applied to me. I was and am a lesbian, and never want to give up my relationships with women for him. So I thought that we were being honest to each other. Now in retrospect I see that I sacrificed too much. I learned a lot, had some great moments, but it all belongs to the past.

Now I myself decide whether I want to tell people about that past. He can't decide. If he didn't want such a story to be told, he should have thought about it seven years earlier. Then he should have taken up with another woman, not me. It isn't my aim to harm him with this story. My aim is to provide some insight into the unperceived inequality which rapidly slips into a priest-woman relationship.

My decision is a firm one: I never want a relationship with a man or priest or woman who doesn't dare to be open about his or her relationship with me.

That's what I've learned.

Greetje

Greetje responded to a newspaper article. She had only talked to a doctor and then very superficially. 'First you must tell me whether you're a Catholic, and if so to what degree,' he had told her.

She was the only girl in a family of four brothers, and was ten when her youngest brother was born. Now she is living with him, fifty-one years after his birth. He drinks too much, just as her father did.

All her life she has looked after others. First her brother, then her mother and later her father. In between came the chaplain. That lasted about eight years. She had imagined something different there.

She was born in 1927. Life was good. As the only daughter she often had a good time with her mother. The war period cast a shadow because during this period her father couldn't keep away from other women and all too often went for the bottle. Her mother fell sick when she was fifty. 'Gradually it got worse. I gave up my courtship because I had to stay and look after mother.'

When she was eighteen her parents divorced. 'I sat between them in court.' And so it went on; she was always sitting between people who needed her support. Things had to be very bad for people in their fifties in a Catholic family to think of divorce. Moreover mother said, 'Before God I am married to you.' It was a divorce of table and bed.

When Greetje was thirty-five her father came back home. He had cancer. She can still describe it in detail, all these years later. 'I couldn't, O God, I couldn't, but I had to.' She looked after both her father and her mother. There was a deathbed reconciliation. 'Father, will you give mother your hand?' she asked. When mother said that all was well her father died.

Greetje continued to look after her mother. The chaplain came regularly to visit her mother. Perhaps more often than to the other sick people. On one occasion he said to Greetje, 'May I give you a kiss?', and Greetje said yes. She found him charming and she had noticed that he often came to greet her during the mass. When he visited her mother he always also talked with her afterwards in the kitchen. During one of these conversations he said that he would have preferred to be a religious education teacher. One day he came back from upstairs and went to the kitchen where Greetje was busy. 'I want to talk to you, but coffee first.' He could command her. 'What do I mean to you? I want an answer?' Greetje didn't answer his question, but asked him what she meant to him. 'Everything, I swear.' He held her tight and touched her body. 'He was quite crazy, feeling all over.' He would come back often. It got more and more difficult for Greetje. She was alone, looking after her mother. The chaplain was there almost every day. For whom, for her? But what attention for her? Was it only her body he wanted?

When she was telling her story, it didn't come over well. Two people who were driven to each other in loneliness? What did she then know of sex? She was forty, but had always looked after her mother, had no friends. And he was forty-five, but what had the seminary taught him about his own feelings?

Greetje told me how 'fraught' he was; there was no talk of her feelings nor did she think of them. It went on like that for a time. He came often, very often, and then touched her all over. Often this gave him a spontaneous ejaculation, and sometimes he asked her to finish him off. And Greetje did what was asked for her. Just as she had looked after her brother and later her father and her mother, so she also saw to the needs of the chaplain.

What did she herself receive? Perhaps some attention, some humanity and the feeling that someone cares a bit for you. On various occasions he asked her to come to his monastery to 'consider' what should happen. First she didn't go, but later she did. That was after he told her, 'I have nocturnal ejaculations, you must lie with me on the cushion.' He pushed her to the ground and opened his trousers. There was no more than a premature ejaculation. 'He was very afraid that something would come of it, that I would get pregnant.' She resolved to go to the monastery to ask for advice. 'I want to talk to a father for whom nothing is too crazy,' she said. She was directed to the caravan chaplain, and she told him everything. She went back home with the advice that her chaplain should leave the church. But he didn't agree. He asked for a move.

While Greetje was telling her story her birds were fluttering in her room: 'The church also suffered. He couldn't do his work well. I don't understand how he could live like that, it wasn't right. At noon he was standing feeling me in the kitchen and in the evening it was "The Lord be with you".' She also told him that. He replied, 'I can't help it if your faith is greater than mine.' She tells how he went away, was moved to another parish. She didn't want to say good-bye. She remained behind with mixed feelings. On the one hand this strange double life was now over, but on the other the only person who had been interested in her had gone away. She cried.

'It was always passion with him. But he didn't want to leave the priesthood, wanted to go on having this status in his family's eyes.'

The chaplain began in his new parish, without Greetje.

After six months he telephoned: would she forget and forgive? Then she said, 'Do you know what you've done? You've ruined my body and profited from my suffering. I can never forget or forgive. I never, never want to see you again.'

Later her mother died. 'When I lost mother, I lost everything.' She later heard from a neighbour that it was a good thing that this chaplain had gone: he played around too much with women. Greetje kept quiet. She had never talked about it with anyone but this doctor.

'Life no longer has any meaning for me,' was the way she ended her story. 'I no longer have the church, that's over.' Sometimes she tries to play the organ which is in her room. And she looks after her brother. That's a major task; he drinks a lot.

After this conversation she told me how sad she is, but also that it had done her good to be able to tell her story.

No tender love

Once there was an old woman in China who had been looking after a monk for more than twenty years. She had built a hut for him and brought him food while he was meditating.

Eventually she wanted to know what progress he had made in all this time. To get to know this she enlisted the help of a girl who had strong desires. 'Go and embrace him,' she said to her, 'and then suddenly ask him, "Now what?"'

The girl went to visit the monk, began to kiss him without further ado and asked him what he was going to do now. 'An old tree grows on a cold rock in winter,' the monk replied somewhat poetically, 'nowhere is there any warmth.' The girl went back and reported what he had said. 'And to think that I've been giving this scoundrel food for twenty years,' exclaimed the old woman in anger. 'Your need for love left him indifferent, he didn't once take the trouble to think of your position. He didn't need to react to your passion, but he could at least have shown some compassion.' She went straight back to the monk's hut and set fire to it.

From Zen-zin, zen-onzin

I don't regret loving

She is sixty-seven and 'her priest' once said to her, 'I will never leave you in the lurch.' That was years ago. It seems as if these words come from another world. After years of sorrow, the suffering of a double life and rejection by her family, the accusations that she led him astray, she's a broken woman. Now she's lost everything: husband, priest-friend and lover, family and friends.

When he was six, his mother died. He was fourteen when she came into his family, first as a friend and later as the wife of his older brother. In that motherless family she also took care of the younger children a bit, including him. 'Then he was just a younger brother. I gave him money and also sometimes bought clothes for him.'

Mara had six children. The priest brother-in-law was always in and out of the family house. Mara was married to his brother. If you were a priest, it was nice to have a home when you came back to the Netherlands on leave. One evening he asked her: 'I've never seen a naked woman. Will you undress for me?' She had known him for years and she wasn't shy.

That's how it began. He fell in love with her. But Mara felt that this was impossible. She talked about it with her husband and said that they were in love with each other. The three sat round the table. Her husband found a solution. He put one of his brother's hands on the table, put his own hand above it and then put Mara's hand in between the two male hands. And so for years Mara was caught between the two men: a husband who drank and a priest who loved her when it pleased him. 'It's very difficult to be two men's woman. I had lots of anxiety and bouts of crying. I didn't know which way to turn. I was constantly on tenterhooks, afraid of an outburst.'

She kept saying to her husband that she no longer wanted this triangular relationship, but her husband did nothing, so she had to put up with it. And Mara did so, because she had been brought up a good Catholic and knew that men must have the say in this life.

It was only much later that she was strong enough to break her fetters. The growing up of her children helped her here. She went to the vicar and told him the situation. 'If he wants, he can and may remain a priest, but you must stop this.' And that is what happened to this servant of the church, the church of her God. Mara struggled through. She left her husband, who could only use her as an unpaid housekeeper and now and then sought to satisfy his sexual feelings on her. He drank too much. Didn't he feel guilty? 'No. He felt that he was the one who was suffering; he had to feel that everything was all right, for the sake of peace.' Once he was without her help he seemed to be in a mess. Was she then important for him? Did he still love her? Did he even need her? Mara was confused about her guilt feelings. Who was now responsible for what? The great absentee from this inner struggle was the priest-lover.

After he had lived abroad for a time, and they had even both been to see him on vacation, he decided to live near her. He found a parish. He invited his beloved when it suited him. Made love with her and gave some warmth to her life. It wasn't much, but Mara wasn't used to even that and it suited him well. But his life was always so full of journeys and courses, especially abroad. He was successful in all this, above all with women. He wasn't a bad lover. 'The sex between us was particularly nice and good. We were considerate of each other. He knew how to treat me, he seemed to have had much more experience. Or perhaps he had read more about it.' After living alone for a bit she returned to her husband. He couldn't manage without her. The priest had suddenly had enough. 'He suddenly wanted to be free, it couldn't go on like this. So my husband could have me back again. He was finished with me, had enjoyed enough. There were plenty of younger women.' Clearly it had all become too burdensome and too complicated for him. A family which knows what is going on, a vicar who leaves you in the lurch. Soon afterwards her husband fell sick and died. Then Mara was completely alone. Some members of the family supported her, others ignored her. On family anniversaries she still meets him. But he seems to have forgotten it all, is an 'ordinary' priest again. At least that's what he pretends. His life goes on as usual. Mara's life is shattered. She still misses him every day. 'He had lots of good points. He showed his love and concern for me by always being there. In good days and in bad he was a great support, not only for me but for the family.' When I asked her to write what properties he most valued in her, she wrote the following: 'My "good" properties were that I began to love him so much. That I gave him all he needed, even my own body. That was a great deal, at least to my mind.' She wrote 'good' in quotation marks, as if she was asking herself whether these characteristics were good. About the first time they went to bed together she wrote: 'If you love each other, making love is great, something that belongs. That was our experience.' Until suddenly she was no longer needed. 'I was left in the lurch. I found that very hard. I loved him a lot.'

It was also a blow to her faith. 'We talked about the faith a lot. We could find each other there, it was nice and worthwhile. My husband had more or less put his faith aside years ago. He no longer went to church, so I also missed that in him.' Her husband was a good father to the children, but a quiet partner. He never said much, even when she crept across the landing at night, from their room to the room where the priest brother-in-law slept. 'I crept through my own house like a thief in the night, squeaking doors, getting cold, in a word shivering. But my husband didn't say anything. That made me very tense.' But hadn't he arranged the triangular relationship in which she lived? Surely he had given his blessing to her priest brother-in-law? 'He was the one who thought that he could arrange things as he liked. Even married life, or what went for it at that time.' She felt more left in the lurch by her priest than by anyone. He should have known better, could have known better. 'His being a priest is worthless. He only wants to be important. He was always too preoccupied with himself, didn't want to lose his standing as a priest. And he still has that standing. As though nothing had happened, as though he had never said, "I'll never leave you in the lurch."' She was sad about many things that had happened, but she also knew that she had really loved: 'I don't regret loving.'

Without a name

For years now I have had a relationship with a priest. More than twenty years. For the first two years of our relationship we lived apart. During this time we talked a lot about how to go on. Our love for each other grew and the need to get married became stronger and stronger. We both had difficulty with the fact that my friend would have to stop his priestly work if we got married. We thought and think that the coupling of priesthood and celibacy is out of date and can no longer be maintained.

During the early years of our relationship it even looked as if this uncoupling would come about in the Dutch church province.

We saw each other more and more often. This led to gossip by some people. After two years my friend got another post in the church. It was then possible for him to have a housekeeper who according to episcopal guidelines should be paid. I then began to live with him as a 'housekeeper'. That had a number of consequences: to begin with I tried to do this alongside my work. It was too much, and I gave up my work. The salary that I got from this time on as a housekeeper was precisely half the salary that I had earned previously. But this was no problem for us. My salary and that of my friend together were enough to get by on.

In addition to my job as housekeeper at the moment I'm doing a lot of work in the diaconate and with church groups. All this gives me a significant place within the local church. To begin with this was difficult: when we lived together and I was just a 'housekeeper', I didn't count anywhere. The voluntary work has changed all that. Of course it was impossible to introduce myself as a priest's woman. No one really knows about our relationship. There are some priest colleagues with whom we have regular contact and with whom we also go on holiday. I think that they understand our relationship, but they've never talked about it.

And we also know about their relationships, but we never talk openly about them either. We feel safe with one another, and that's enough for them. When we go on vacation we sleep in separate rooms, since sooner or later you will meet guests that you know in the hotel. In such matters you must take account of outsiders.

To begin with we both had some difficulty over the fact that in our situation we couldn't have children. But now that time is past. We are happy with one another and no longer miss the fact that we have no children. In retrospect I must say that it's good to have done this. My friend is a very good priest; he enjoys pastoral work and is well qualified. It would be a pity if he had to give it up.

That, briefly, is our story. For reasons of confidentiality I shall send this letter without a name or address. We needed to share this with you. Success for your work. We think you're brave to do it. Warmest greetings.

What a course can lead to

After some weeks I came to the conclusion that I was really madly in love with this dark-haired man. But a lot of water was to flow under the bridge before it came to anything. And now as I write, four years later, this fine dream is already in fragments.

Martin and I did the same course in pastoral work outside our working hours. I knew him vaguely from before. He lived and worked in a centre on the other side of the city. An absorbing pastoral job, a timetable that was just about manageable and high expectations made the atmosphere quite exciting from the start. We were attracted to each other by the counselling exercises in the course. Slowly we began to talk about our work, our ups and downs; we asked each other critical questions and supported each other where necessary. Mutual trust developed. After a holiday it proved that we had missed each other a lot. The first year of the course ended with a party. We danced and didn't say a word. His birthday was ten days later. I summoned up all my courage, bought champagne roses – red were all too obvious – and rang on his doorbell in the evening. Evidently I wasn't the only one to have remembered his birthday. Some of his parishioners looked at me suspiciously. I carefully hid the roses. I blushed like a teenager on a date. But I only needed to ask half a question. That Saturday evening, after the eucharist, we said a lot of other things to each other. Very honestly, openly, in a fragile way, afraid, we gave each other kisses, our hands intertwined and we enjoyed caressing each others' bodies gently. In the morning, around six I had to disappear. I went home rumpled – note that we had lain there all night with our clothes on – and confused.

That evening wasn't the beginning of a 'living together apart'. It was more a matter of 'living apart together'. On the religious level we experienced an exodus: God, human beings, society, liturgy, we saw it all more deeply. We sometimes prepared the Sunday sermon together. We wove the difficulties of an everyday faith tightly into the history of the Christian community and contrasted recent theological conclusions with older, Roman views. Centimetre by centimetre we sounded each other out in the religious sphere. For me the unity in our thought also expressed itself physically. Bodily gestures supplemented words. For me it was years since I had been so one in heart, spirit and body with anyone. My physical freedom was perhaps all too unexpected for Martin. The slow reconnaissance became a policy of centimetres: 'We can go so far and no further'. It was inevitable that the frontier was shifted further every evening. On the one hand Martin felt that the physical language ran parallel to the everyday language, and on the other he began to see that the 'ultimate' was not so ultimate. You can lose your virginity in different ways. The purely physical side isn't the main thing.

After this first part of the story someone might say, 'How splendid!' But to be honest, it wasn't so splendid. However, I only realize that now.

I constantly had to be on my guard. No stroking his hair, no spontaneous kiss, no passing touch. Even my glances were already dangerous. 'Someone might see something.' By 'someone', in the first instance he meant those on the course and the lecturer. Later this 'someone' stood for those living in the centre and his friends. He didn't make it easy for me. When I moved and was busy painting my bathroom, he suddenly appeared, with a friend. Just like that. Remember that we were supposed to know each other only from the course. Or there was the time when I stood at his door with a box of hyacinth bulbs and his older sister happened to be there, 'Yes, madam, the pastor asked for them!' All these situations had to be sorted out. It was more difficult when someone – quite exceptionally, of course – came in after midnight and I was still there. You could say, 'But you shouldn't have gone there at night', but that was the only time when we could talk and caress each other undisturbed. We always spent Friday evenings like this, and it was also sometimes possible on Saturday evenings.

Going home was sometimes a job. 'Are they all asleep? Can you hear anyone? Is there still a light on?' The mere slamming of a door gave us grey hairs. We never knew for certain whether anyone saw us. Outside, Martin would go to the car and I to the corner of the street; there he picked me up and took me to my house. We got to bed around three or four. He to his and I to mine. I needn't explain how much energy this took. Once we were so tired that we just fell asleep together, and then we woke in the morning in a panic.

Of course this constant loss of sleep didn't help the balance between pastoral work and the relationship. If for example a preparatory talk before a marriage went well – because we had spent hours over it – that was normal. If a sermon went wrong – through too little sleep – that was a minus for the relationship.

'Either the parish or the relationship', I was often told. Martin ultimately didn't seem able to accept a combination. He suffered under either one or the other. It seemed to me that it was always a matter of protecting his priestly choice. Suppose that a relationship didn't get in the way of exercising a priestly office, indeed that pastoral and official work were more integrated by a relationship, why still maintain a difference between priests and laity, unmarried and married? This protection and setting apart of the priestly caste was of course encouraged by the psychological and physical output that we had to provide almost every day. The idea that life, our life, would be in a sense livable if our best friends and our families were to know, never occurred to Martin.

'Officially', friends and parents still know nothing. Then, a year after it all began, Martin was offered an exchange. For health reasons an old friend had to give up his parish in Surinam for a while and was looking for a replacement for a couple of years. Martin went off to Surinam. Accepting his decision caused me much sadness.

There was an impressive correspondence. We sent miles of airmail letters. Everything, but everything, came out on paper. Serious discussions, unpunctuated discourses, tears and perfumes, banalities. It was splendid. The relationship got firmer and more intense. I rose above any sadness. We made plans for the future. I would fly over after a year. How anxious and happy I was when

I arrived in that warm land after an eleven-hour flight. Our eyes spoke volumes. Those were honeymoon weeks. Unforgettable. I was the happiest woman in the world. I came back radiant. We would make it.

We never did. When Martin took the decision to come back to the Netherlands I began to ask quite practical questions like: 'Shall we meet in a more normal way? Can we agree fixed days and nights? Shouldn't we tell our best friends and families? What do you think of a week in the Wadden Islands in June?' I didn't want to lead an incognito life. Was I asking too much? I don't think so. Most of all I would have liked to ask him to marry me. I was already dreaming of a couple of young rascals. A few of my friends have a successful relationship with a priest, why couldn't this happen for us?

In our letters this became the central problem. I hurt him, he hurt me. The old discussion flared up again: can a priest share his life with anyone without his parish suffering? There was no answer to this question. It was the 'parents and friends' who made him capitulate. It would disappoint them. And me? I could continue to love him. And I do. But I've put a stop to it. I don't want someone who can't choose, who doesn't have the courage to come out with his love.

After four years I've put an end to our relationship. I let him go without rancour. He's a splendid priest. I fear that he will be lonely, that slowly he will wear himself out, that his life for and in the church will become unliveable, that sooner or later his parish will suffer. He needs me, but I'm not a charitable institution which only gives and never asks for anything. I'm a woman and I've never loved anyone more than him.

My friend

Now he looks down with a happy glow,
   and smiles with God on these fools below.
He has his own ideas about the Lord,
   tralalala, his own ideas.

1957-1978

The story that I tell here is my story. It is my truth. The one who
lived out this story with me is no more. He can no longer provide
a commentary on it.

It is 1957, Lent (for the 'heathen' among you, the forty days
before Easter), and I am fifteen. My favourite cousin, almost my
second mother, is staying with us in Breda. The telephone rings
and an unforgettable voice asks for Jos, my cousin.
   That is the beginning.

A September night in 1978.
   A man dies.
   I finally write the text of the advertisment which has already
been going through my head for months. Before this moment I
dared not write these words, afraid that I might hasten his end
with them. I write: 'My friend is dead. He is finally free.'

1957-1978: a young girl who becomes a grown woman and a
man at the height of his development who sees his star set too
early.

Not so long ago my German teacher said to me, 'You were a nail
in my coffin, you didn't open your mouth.' This characteristic has

been useful to me. At that moment I didn't sense it, but in retrospect the great silence began in 1957.

The facts

It was no very loving family that I came from: in other words, for me there was love enough – I was the youngest – but there was also plenty of conflict.

In his first marriage father had had a dependent and willing wife; mother, father's second wife, good at talking and good at learning, had led an independent life until she was forty. Just imagine it! Moreover this woman, my mother, bore him three pig-headed daughters in a row, so that the women's front was complete.

Because I wanted to study music (piano) and wanted to get away from all the fuss at home and because my cousin Jos lived in The Hague and appeared to work for this intriguing man with that voice, in 1959 on a summery but misty morning I cycled from Breda to The Hague to live there. The trunk with my luggage – at seventeen you don't have much – came on by carrier.

At last real life began. Not so much through the remarkable people who lived in that guest-house in Balistraat (the old man who wouldn't hear a word against his comrade Prince Hendrik; the pianist who had seen a career go up in smoke as a result of a blackout during a recital), as through the comings and goings of celebrities and semi-celebrities around my cousin. I had the feeling that I was involved in one big adventure and I would do anything to be present everywhere, preferably standing in front.Peeling potatoes, pouring coffee, vacuum cleaning, washing cars, typing – I didn't mind. And I also studied the piano: on a splendid grand piano in a splendid house on the Frankenslag.

Socially speaking, up to the moment when I arrived in The Hague, Piet's life had gone very well: he had a radio programme which had done well for years, 'This is Life', and as a result of that a flourishing lecture circuit, the annual climax of which were Lenten meditations in various cities which attracted great crowds. But in that very year 1959 things began to decline: the radio programme was dropped, he himself saw the Lenten meditations tailing off, and the simmering professional jealousy among his brethren began to become rather more venomous. Some wanderings began in which Jos – and initially I – followed him loyally: Noordwijker-hout, Nijmegen. I made a first attempt to detach myself, for no matter how implicit everything still was at that time, there was something going on that – in just as unconscious and unacknowleged a way – I was afraid of.

I moved to Amsterdam and then to Paris. When I had a week's holiday in the Netherlands, Piet let me know that he had missed me a lot. On my return to Paris I found a letter from Iceland saying that he hadn't meant it like that and that I was to forget our conversation. That was 1962, I was almost twenty-one and very confused.

Back permanently in the Netherlands I went to live with my cousin Jos again, this time in Nijmegen. A bet that got somewhat out of hand led to my enrolling in the faculty of law. This time, living with Jos was not a success. A provincial girl of seventeen is rather easier than a woman of twenty-one from Paris used to her own way. In addition, my attitude to Piet caused much offence: in my eyes he could do no wrong. Jos moved to Doorn and I went too, until my sister who got me on the telephone in tears for the umpteenth time intervened and said that it was time for me to live on my own. That was a sensible remark and two months later I was sitting profoundly content in an attic room in Nijmegen without a cousin keeping an eye on me.

It was my second, apparently rather more successful, attempt at escape. At any rate, this time I was making a real life of my own and in my own way I misbehaved: singing in the café with lots of beer (too much), going out with strange types, sleeping instead of going to college, walking all over the place in the middle of the night. My relationship with Piet was very unclear. He was sometimes there and sometimes not. Other men were interested in me – yes, including two theologians.

The turning point came in 1966 when Piet was appointed pastor in Spijkenisse with the task of building a church there. Of course he couldn't be a pastor with a woman friend, he told me. I immediately got myself a steady boy-friend. But that wasn't the intention. Piet panicking and me in tears. In February 1967 Piet went on holiday with Jos to Tunisia where she finally resolved to get married (to a sculptor in Laren). I got Pfeiffer's disease and broke off the relationship with my boy friend. After Piet's return I convalesced in Spijkenisse. We saw that we couldn't go on without each other. After my period of sickness – it lasted six months in all – a kind of weekend marriage came about. During the week I studied and lived in Nijmegen, and at weekends I went to Spijkenisse. I liked that very much. My Nijmegen life grew and flourished and was a good compensation for the completely different, somewhat heavier, life in Spijkenisse. My best friends came there for the weekend now and then, never asked questions, understood everything, even what went unsaid. New friendships arose in Spijkenisse as well.

I was no longer so breathless with admiration for my idol; I was difficult and critical. A friend from this time said to me on his death: 'You were never afraid of Piet; I admired that.' When she was twenty-five, an adolescent of fifteen could accept that the object of her admiration proved to be a man of flesh and blood. A man with a great talent and the qualities which went with it: convinced that he was right, rebellious, and blessed with a great sense of humour.

That I could make this leap was probably largely thanks to (or the fault of!) my loyalty, which above all was reminiscent of the doggedness of a terrier. But the most important thing was that Piet was such a fascinating person. 'They must have news to report' was how a friend recently summed it up for me. Yes, they do have news to report. And Piet had news to report: stories, true or fantasies; views that you could or couldn't oppose; visions of the future that you could or couldn't share in. And above all plans, constantly new plans and crazy ideas which usually led nowhere, but sometimes produced a fascinating interview or brought interesting speakers to a temporary church in Spijkenisse. Of the interviews the one with Cardinal Ottaviani on his retirement was the most notorious, and the speakers I can still remember are especially Godfried Bomans, Harry Mulisch and Hans van Mierlo. In short, it was all very dynamic.

My mother died at this time. She had told me on the telephone what text she wanted on her memorial notice: '*In te, domine, speravi, non confundar in aeternum*' (In thee, O Lord, have I trusted, let me never be confounded). Thanks to the fact that Piet had once visited my parents, I could suggest to the family that he should conduct her funeral service.

Otherwise I had avoided contacts between Piet and my family. My father and mother asked no questions, and my brothers, scattered all over the world, scarcely knew that I existed. Of my two sisters, only the interfering one had to be taken into account, and she had gone to Africa.

With Pfeiffer's disease behind me, my mother dead, and a failed examination, my doctor told me that now I really must go to work. He was right. Within a very short space of time I did the first part of my master's degree; it proved rather less easy to get the second part. A well-known Dutch politician saw to it that I failed. What cheek! Two other well-known people had been satisfied with me in the first part of my examination. Finally, after the coldest and longest winter that I can remember, in March 1970 I got my degree and could call myself Master of Law. They called me mistress in Spijkenisse; what would they mean by that now?

On 24 March 1970 I got my coveted piece of paper, on 25 March I gave notice to move and from 1 May I was permanently living in Spijkenisse in a new house that Piet had got for himself shortly beforehand. A new chapter had begun.

Neither of us had any experience of living together, that is to say, words living together without the possibility of escape. When Piet was practically living in Doorn with Jos he always in fact had a room in a monastery somewhere, and when I spent each weekend in Spijkenisse, I knew that I could always return to my cold room in Nijmegen on the second floor back.

So there were conflicts. My first worry was, how do I get a job? Piet's first worry was, who does the housework? I had no intention of making coffee and tea for all the church people who kept coming and going. Piet was used to having this done for him. He could sometimes express views with which I heartily disagreed and then I shouted out loud and clear, visitors or not. Priests are brought up with the illusion that they have the truth and that any contradiction is to be refuted, and not listened to.

Piet found things difficult, really from the moment that he had settled in Spijkenisse. As he himself said; 'I used to give a nice sermon to a full church and after that I got happily into my car without knowing what I had caused.' And now he himself wanted nothing more than contact with his parishioners, if only because there he at last found the ordinary human warm-heartedness that he had never experienced in all those monasteries the last few years. Only the parishioners not only gave warmth, but also an uncensored commentary. They confronted him with their daily existence, which there was no chance of fitting into all those church rules. For Piet, Spijkenisse represented a turning point in his development, in his life. He was well aware that he had taken leave of all kinds of glamour in an upsurge of heroics. And what did he get in return? Rebellious parishioners. But he learned, and learned quickly. When you think that Piet began this adventure in his fiftieth year, it was a miracle. A couple of weeks after Paul VI issued his encyclical *Humanae Vitae* in 1968, Piet gave his own account of sex, marriage and contraception. The message amounted to: 'Go by your conscience'. Despite their growing self-awareness, there were still many people who were enlightened by what he said; they still needed this support against the pope of Rome. And now as well as the rebellious parishioners he had a woman who knew her own mind in his house.

Despite my feeling of living in a glass house, in retrospect I had resolved not to lose myself. Quite apart from the career problem – it took me almost nine months to find a good job – there was a culture which Piet himself had produced in the parish as a result of which everyone felt justified in concerning themselves with our life and above all with our household. Almost always the intentions were good – quite often this involvement came just at the right time, but all too often I had to defend myself against people who came to take over the show. Women and men who thought that my way of housekeeping wasn't any good. It may not have been, but it was *my* way. You had to explain the unusual set-up of the house to people. In addition there was a church committee that really thought Piet a strange and above all irresponsible man with a troublesome woman in the house.

Still, it was quite strange – and my amazement at this has hardly lessened after all these years – that my presence in the house was generally accepted. For years I had been coming to see Piet each weekend and now I was living with him. There was certainly a good deal of talk (but not to me); however, the general tendency was: 'That's much better. Such a man shouldn't be alone.' For events, birthdays, the two of us were always invited together and if Piet dared to come without me he had to justify himself. 'Where is Tinus?' Nevertheless, Piet tried to conceal me, even in the period when my presence could hardly be denied any more. His provincial came for a visitation (a visit, in ordinary language) and I wasn't very keen on being sent out to eat with friends from whom Piet could come and get me when the danger was past.

In addition I still had my own circle: my family, my student friends, my new friends at work. Piet had hardly any part in this and I thought it best. I still kept two lives separate: life with Piet in Spijkenisse, where friends knew and parishioners couldn't help knowing, and my life alone with people who at most suspected something.

At the point when I went to live in Spijkenisse, Piet had already been working there for four years, and while almost everyone took my presence for granted, around that time there was a serious conflict with the church authorities over precisely this question of priests and women.

To explain the situation I should point out that in 1971 the tolerant Bishop Jansen had been followed by the not at all radical chaplain Simonis.

At the end of the 1960s a friend of ours, a married priest, had been presiding over worship in Spijkenisse. The parishioners knew who their pastor was this Sunday and it became a moving occasion. It never got into the newspaper. At the request of the priest involved there was no publicity. It was a matter for Spijkenisse and that was that.

But on Sunday 25 April 1971 Huub Oosterhuis appeared in Spijkenisse. He had married precisely a year earlier, and for that reason was no longer a favourite of Bishop Simonis, although one Oosterhuis hymn after another had been sung at Simonis' consecration the previous month.

Deliberate publicity was given to Huub Oosterhuis's appearance and there was inevitably a reaction. Previously the deacon (= functionary between pastor and bishop, too important to serve, not important enough to celebrate) had threatened Piet on the telephone: he would not be responsible for the consequences if Piet went through with this plan. It turned into a full-blown row and at the same time the beginning of the end. And neither the bishop nor the deacon had to dirty their hands with it. The church council, which was already discontented for all kinds of reasons, supported by between four and ten parishioners, did a hatchet job. On 10 May there was a popular court in the form of an open parish meeting. Under the approving eye of a representative of the diocese Piet was accused of fraud and neglect of duty. An interesting factor was that the same church authority which brought this charge had resolved on the ridiculous initial salary of fl350 a month for Piet, the reason why he had taken another job (teacher of religion at a school in Hoogvliet). The evidence of fraud was very slight, as was the sum in connection with which it was made. Piet was clearly not a pastor who went by the book, which on the one hand meant that he neglected tasks above all in administration, and on the other provided high points on Sunday of which people in Spijkenisse still talk.

I can properly pass over the rest of the story. The stage was set, and everyone played their role as the church had intended. At the end of 1971 Piet gave his mandate back to the diocese. On 26 May 1972 we moved to Voorschoten. The last chapter began.

The fact that he was required to keep silent, the fact that he was socially cut off, the fact that he seemed to have few real friends, all this took its toll of Piet. Before this time he didn't exactly live as a teetotaller; now everyone who dropped in was a good excuse for a large drink. Whereas formerly he could play the role of the murdered innocent and misunderstood genius, now he had a regular depression. *Taedium vitae*, I read in a report that I just happened to see: weariness of life. This weariness of life made him sick. The years in Voorschoten were the years when evening after evening I went back home deeply anxious: what had happened this time?

Whereas my own professional life was making progress – I now worked in the Second Chamber, as I had wanted to for ages – his career was moving to a sorry end. A vigorous and complicated conflict developed at the school where he worked. When the dust-clouds settled, all the teachers involved were dismissed, including Piet. After some bickering it emerged that given his age he had the right to some form of compensation, so that in any case we had no worries over money.

And, as I said, Piet fell sick. After some earlier attacks of stomach cramps our doctor thought it better to admit Piet to hospital for observation. I took him in, and before he knew it he was in intensive care. In February 1975 he underwent a first intestinal operation from which he seemed to recover rapidly. After that it was something every year: in March 1976 an ileus, in March 1977 another operation (a different hospital, a different surgeon); in January 1978 the last operation. Between these incidents the last great happening took place, his sixtieth birthday. All our old and recent friends came just once more for a party. There were lots of flowers, lots of presents, much warmth, the recalling of lots of memories, along with singing and dancing. In short, there was a lot of noise in the inner city.

Meanwhile Piet had managed to get another platform from which to express his thoughts and ideas. A good friend put him in touch with the *Leidsch Dagblad* and he got a contract to write a weekly column. The first appeared in April 1976, when he had just come back from his most recent adventure in the hospital. The last appeared on the day of his death in 1978. These columns were his joy. I can't remember his ever missing a week.

What else is there to say about these last years, about the descending line of life? The hope, the doubt, the certainty? The endless nights? The pain, the anxiety, the tears?

After his last operation in January 1978, which lasted for hours, the surgeon, God bless him, said: 'Piet is dying of intestinal cancer. I've done what I could, I've treated him like a brother, but I can't save him.'

His will-power lengthened his life by a further nine months. He spent three of them in the Rudolf Steiner Clinic. One of the visitors there was the same Bishop Simonis who had shut him up. With a last effort Piet spoke to this wavering man. A deeply moved Simonis left the hospital. Outside he realized once again that he was the bishop.

After three months in the Steiner Clinic Piet wanted to go home. Well-meaning people seriously dissuaded me from my plan. Both hospital and doctor supported me. I would get all the help I needed. And so it was. For six months I looked after Piet with the help of many others. There were farewell visits from every direction. Piet died in the night of 28/29 September. A candle which went out, after that a vigorous presence, a powerful stream of energy. In the course of the night all this slowly ebbed away.

On 4 October we took him away. The service was held in the very place where Piet had celebrated his sixtieth birthday, with similar company. Again there were many flowers, and again much warmth. After it was over my sister (from Africa), my brother-in-law and my friends stayed with me. Plans were made for a weekend in Germany with friends. I took my first cautious steps back to the land of the living.

Ten years later

This story is certainly not complete. Twenty years can't be set down in a few pages. There are doubtless things that I've forgotten. There are things which concern no one. Some dates may be wrong. But the essentials are true, at least for me.

I'm now forty-seven, and I shall try to put into words what these twenty years meant to me.

First of all there was the great difference in age, the twenty-five years which separated us. There was the natural fascination of a girl of fifteen for a much older broadcaster, a famous person in those days. Another thing that made it different was that I didn't go away when the idol proved to be a person with unattractive as well as attractive characteristics. That things went as they did and lasted as long as they did, as far as my involvement was concerned, was a combination of love, stubbornness and compassion. I grew up at an accelerated pace: from a provincial girl to a young woman who knew how to cope with a demanding man. Part of my youth is included in this, but in my 'own' life that I led alongside Piet, I caught it up.

Piet also taught me to talk. In the long run I could routinely answer his slogan, 'Tell me something nice for once' (with which initially he could flatten every attempt at conversation on my part), with anecdotes which I had saved up in my back pocket. It still comes in handy in all kinds of situations when there is an all too threatening silence. But I need only tell myself, 'Say something nice', and a box of stories opens.

What I got rid of was the schoolgirl in me. All the prissiness that I had carefully saved up in seventeen, eighteen years of life didn't seem to fit the unusual situation I found myself in. And struggling against it, I became a forward-looking person who knew what life was about.

Anyway, I didn't for a moment consider persuading Piet to marry me. I was 'not the marrying type', and didn't have such a need to be 'the wife of', but rather went through life on my own. Moreover, if there is something like vocation, then Piet unmistakably had one. It was unthinkable that he would leave the priesthood.

As a result of all that happened in those years I am no longer so anxious. Anxious about the authorities, anxious about sickness, anxious about death, anxious about money, anxious about unexpected situations: I've got rid of some of this anxiety. The situation, the man, made me strong. One can only survive in the proximity of such a powerful personality by making oneself grow. I would never have become what I am now had I not met Piet. On the other hand, I am convinced that certainly after my studies, I had a great influence on him in turn. I can't prove it, it can't be measured, but I'm convinced of that.

Of course there's another side, as there is in any friendship, in any relationship. But the circumstances gave the other side a weight of its own.

To mention one thing, there is the loss of my Roman Catholic youth. Despite the bickering over the books that you couldn't read and the clothing that you had to wear and despite the crushing boredom in church on Sundays, despite all this, Roman

Catholic culture gladdened my youth. I grew up with a joyful belief. That came above all from my mother. She was deeply religious, but she dealt lightly with all these external phenomena. She lived out her faith in a slapdash way, and that delighted me as a child. I lost this joy, first slowly and then, the more I saw behind the scenes in the church, increasingly rapidly. Now, in 1989, I can again look back happily on my Catholic upbringing, sensing that my antipathy exclusively relates to the bare oppression of the institution. I've got rid of the happy naivety for good.

Indeed, and then there is the way in which people, men and women, tend to express their love. I can be brief about this: a man whose sexual education in seminary largely consisted in pictures of female sexual organs in an advanced stage of venereal disease, someone who has undergone such brainwashing, no longer has such an appetite.

And there was always that troublesome third party, the church of Rome. The church of Rome, the church which made a distasteful brew from ecclesiastical greed, contempt for women (doesn't St Thomas ask somewhere whether the woman has a soul?) and frustrated sexuality to legitimate the obligation to celibacy.

What initially was an exciting secret soon became an intolerable burden because I couldn't speak to anyone about Piet. Above all in those first on and off years – sometimes I wasn't even clear whether Piet was or wasn't there – I found myself lost in a solitary wilderness to which I no longer admitted anyone. All those years of solitude culminated in Pfeiffer's disease. Even after that, during the weekend marriage and living together I never discussed my way of life with anyone, not even with dear and trusted friends. To outsiders I always spoke about my 'housemate', as if to create distance.

Only when Piet was dead did I have a first conversation with my sister about what it had been like to live with Piet.

Only when Piet was dead did I write 'my friend'.

Only then did it come through to some people what he had meant to me.

I would dissuade anyone from denying such an important part

86

of their life and pushing it away. I talked about it for seven years, wrote about it for seven years, wept about it for seven years. Then it was finally over; I could at last close the book.

The summing-up is a conclusion which is there from the start.

I would not want to have missed this man, Piet Weisseling, in my life for anything. The experience with him has made me what I am; I am content with my life, content with who I am.

But the fact that I could never make him happy, the fact that I never really knew what I meant to him, makes me say, 'I shall never do this again, never again lead such a life.' The halfness of this life, both socially and personally, doesn't bear repeating.

And so the circle is closed and the story told.

Father Peter

    I sing you the song of Father Peter,
        a pastor of God from the land of Pallieter,
        he had his own ideas about the Lord,
        tralalala, his own ideas.

    He sat in the sun, watched the flowers grow,
        at home in the evening he let the wine flow,
        he had his own ideas about the Lord,
        tralalala, his own ideas.

    Each Sunday the mass was always late,
        he went fishing for pike and for trout with his bait,
        he had his own ideas about the Lord,
        tralalala, his own ideas.

    Those wanting confession would have to wait,
        the laughter that greeted his sermons was great,
        he had his own ideas about the Lord,
        tralalala, his own ideas.

    'This man is no good, doesn't live by the letter,
        he'll end up in hell if he doesn't do better,

he has his own ideas about the Lord,
tralalala, his own ideas.'

Eventually no one would go by his house,
and those still did, made the sign of the cross,
he had his own ideas about the Lord,
tralalala, his own ideas.

A smile, 'Let it be, Lord', and then he was dead.
'He's now gone to hell, God be praised,' people said,
'he had his own ideas about, you, Lord,
tralalala, his own ideas.'

(T.de Verre, as sung by Henk Elsink)

Brigitte

I got to know him on my mother's birthday. He was new in the parish. Because I had left home almost ten years before and no longer followed developments in the parish, I didn't know that he was 'a new one'. But when I saw him, I thought: 'It's nice that for once they've thought of appointing someone younger in such an old traditional area.' Even my mother liked him, so that her Catholic view of 'needs a white beard' had clearly lost its force. He didn't have one. After an introductory conversation, topics which interested me emerged. And I thought, 'You can talk with him, too.' Earlier experiences of 'You shall... you shall not...' from the pulpit had made me stay away from the church and its servants all my youth, to the great sorrow of my mother. Perhaps it was that she now saw a chink of light: to deepen our conversations further it was perhaps a good thing that I should visit him at the clergy house. I don't know precisely what she imagined by this. That it would stop at this one meeting?

There were dozens and dozens. After two and half years we lived together. And I still didn't go to church... The initial period was stormy in the family circle. My father, brothers and sisters looked on it somewhat oddly to begin with, but they didn't exert any presure. My mother was cross. How could I, how dare I, 'seduce' a priest? When I once answered that it took at least two for this she stopped talking to me for a long time. Later we talked it out, though at that moment 'the shame' in her eyes did not disappear. Now, after years, the storm has abated and you could speak of cautious acceptance.

It wasn't easy for me, either. I was glad to have found someone who wanted to share love and sorrow with me, as I with him. And I still am. I wouldn't want to be without him. But your surroundings change, also by your own doing. You don't depend on the great thing that you're living with a priest. You're cautious outside. Your contacts grow less because you're afraid of saying too much. You aren't anxious about the 'scandal' that it could be talked about. That's your own choice. What you are anxious about is that you can take so much away from the life of your partner if the relationship is discovered. From one moment to the next he then no longer counts; with the congregation, in the church sphere, even in his own family.

In the course of these years I've seen various priests 'killed off'. Hard-working, dedicated people, who were putting into practice what they had always been asked to do: love for fellow human beings. Only this fellow human being was a woman.

Another consequence of the association was that I came into contact with other religious. To begin with I wasn't at all enthusiastic. I still hadn't much time for 'church people' and the church, however contradictory that may sound for someone with a priest as partner. But here too you make your own choices, although this took me some time. Brought up traditionally, as a woman I was always taught to be there for the man: to share his life, his work, to accept his life and friends as your own. Sometimes you have to leave the work of educators as it is...

The few people who remain and with whom you have a good relationship aren't always enough as a background to your life. As a 'priest's woman in secret' you're very much alone. And not only the woman, but the priest. I know some married priests and their women. They too have such experiences, but their world is freer, more ordinary, less tense. And their reaction is often 'Why don't you get married?'

But it's not as simple as that. Anyone who has a priest as partner, as I do, will be able to understand why.

A special kind of 'flu

I got to know him at a meeting of Amnesty International. We clearly were there out of the same interest. A friendship developed. He came to visit me and we discovered that we had much in common. I found that as time went on he began to fall in love. 'Is that possible for a priest?' I asked myself. But I also found him very attractive. He was attentive, and above all the conversations we had together were a revelation to me. I could talk to him easily. Often he would telephone me, 'just to talk'. He showed that he had a special interest in me. Once he stayed until late into the night. Then we slept together. I found that tremendous. He wasn't a fantastic lover immediately, but loving and attentive. That's how it began. After we had gone to bed together for the first time, we talked a lot: was our relationship possible? But he constantly reassured me. Explained to me that his vocation, his priesthood, was the most important thing for him and would remain so. But we lived in modern times. I had definitely no need to marry anyway. I was very content with our relationship as it now was. It inspired me, brought colour to my life; I thought it fantastic that here was someone who gave me so much. And I gave to him. My 'ordinary' life went on normally. I understood that I couldn't talk about this with anyone; you had to keep quiet about it. Other people would find it crazy and wouldn't understand. There was something good between us and that didn't concern anyone.

I had a demanding career and found much satisfaction in it. He came a couple of times a week, we talked long and much, often listened to music and then spent the night together, after making long and passionate love. He learned much about sex from me. Learned how nice it can be, unburdened by guilt. He was really very sensual, very passionate. He often moaned with pleasure when I caressed him. He was quite different from the men I had known earlier in my life. A gentle man, you could say. And he could listen to my stories, my questions and the things that attracted me in life. I hadn't noticed that earlier.

Sometimes he had difficulties with his own life. Then he said that monastic life had caved in so much. No one knew the old values any longer and the new forms didn't appeal to him. He interpreted celibacy in his own way: you had to remain available for everyone. A relationship with someone of the kind we had (at that time he called it a unique friendship) was possible. As long as it didn't endanger his calling. We both took care about that. We were very careful. I understood him well. Sometimes it was difficult, but there was so much on the other side: our great walks in the country, our good conversations and our intimacy, our physical love. Meanwhile he had become better and better as a lover. Really it was very good. Then it wasn't such a burden that our relationship had to remain secret. I took it as an extra. I also accepted that often he had no time, or that we couldn't meet because his work had priority. I carefully protected the good things that we did have and cherished them. Took care that we experienced this regularly. In short, as we told each other, it was all very nice.

After a few years it proved that he was also sharing these nice things with other women. That was a great shock. He didn't see why this shouldn't be possible. That was the breaking point: I began to ask myself what our relationship meant to him. Perhaps those meetings he went to were one of these other women. And what about the uniqueness of our relationship? I was shattered. And again I told no one. Went on with my work as usual. Was alone at home for a week 'with 'flu' – but surely that can happen to anyone?

I also spent many hours making clear to myself what the situation really was: had he really been honest with me? In that case, why did he need relations with other women? I got no answer to this. He certainly showed me that his life was really a wreck. Monastic life didn't really give him the fulfilment that he sought. Our relationship had become close. Really he was a bungler, confused in his own life: about his sense of God, his ideas of monastic life and his relations with women. He thought that he was just doing good. I no longer needed him. Never saw him again. Later I heard that he had gone abroad.

I've thought a lot about how our relationship collapsed. We were on the way to becoming intimate partners. I think that it was the intimacy that he found threatening. It was easier for him if everything remained on the outside. That was how he had been brought up. I was just seeking intimacy, being attuned to each other, letting yourself be known by the other, being vulnerable. If you make this choice it also means that you can be easily wounded by your partner, although you know that he didn't mean it like that. But that's the only way in which real intimacy can arise. He was looking for something different in his relations with people. Something different from me. So it went wrong. And I got a special kind of 'flu.

Magda

Magda is a member of a congregation of women religious.

Relationships also occur within the walls of convents. Perhaps people are even more silent about them there. Silent in a certain sense: to have a friend, male or female, is permissible and even good for a person, but there is never any talk about just what this relationship is. The intensity of such relationships is kept secret.

Magda wanted to talk about it. She thinks that the double morality which a number of priests have towards women does no good. Behind the 'having to be there for many people' there is often a lack of love in early youth, a strong bond to the mother and the feeling of being a special person. So special that you can even make special demands on your partner. Demands which are sometimes impossible.

Magda finally also made demands herself: she wanted clarity. In a good relationship partners can say what does and does not feel good. Magda said that. In the end it cost her the relationship. The way that you then have to take is a difficult one and you are often completely alone. Magda told her story not only for herself, but also for others.

The story of the denial

'About eighteen months ago I broke off my relationship with Simon. How did the relationship begin and in what circumstances? What did I feel about it and how did I grow in it? What were the difficulties, the pain and the sorrow which ultimately led to my breaking off the relationship after twenty years? And what does it mean for me to have to go on "alone"?

In the middle of the 1950s, at the age of twenty, I entered a

94

congregation of active women religious. It was a time when the fixed rules and customs of years still seemed natural, though in retrospect the signs of crisis were already becoming evident and attempts were being made to bring religious life "up to date".

A virginal life played a great role, the vow to chastity and to remain unmarried. It meant that I could give myself undividedly to God so as to be available to many people. It also meant that I could not cherish any friendship or preference for anyone at all.

When I think back on those first ten years in the convent, it strikes me that I didn't experience many really high or low points. That was possibly because in this period I seldom had any authentic, deeply human contacts. Only in subsequent years did I feel and experience this for the first time, in contact with Simon.

In 1965, when the renewal and deepening in the world of religious was well under way, I had the chance to go and study theology. There was a quest for the original sources of inspiration and a new formation, in which new content was also given to the vows. Ideas about friendship and affection also fitted into this new view, which developed further in the course of the 1970s.

This time of change caused me some tension. I had a function in the governing body of the congregation; I was young and felt torn between the conservative group and the younger members of the congregation, who thought that I should support them and take a stand in favour of the renewal. In this difficult period I met Simon at a meeting which he was in charge of. He was a few years older, and was himself also a member of a religious order. Among other things he was responsible for directing renewal within orders and congregations. He had prepared himself for this by schooling and training, and along with others he tried out new methods, like sensitivity training, to bring groups to a deeper level of praying and believing. This often gave rise to deep human relationships. In the personal discussion which followed the meeting, I found Simon a sensitive man, full of understanding and personal involvement. His dedication to the renewal of religious life attracted me a lot.

As a result of his particularly warm way of greeting people, in which I experienced more physical contact than I was used to with men, my feeling of attraction towards him began to grow. At first I didn't want to acknowledge this and doubted whether it would fit in with my religious life. The feeling of loving him and tension about what it would do to him released much in me. Feelings of happiness, but also of powerlessness and helplessness. After some hesitation I expressed these feelings. He assured me that he also loved me and we came to the joint decision to seek a way for this budding friendship. What came first was that we both wanted to remain faithful to the order and congregation in which we were actively involved. The rest we left more or less open.

The beginning of our relationship was marked by some inequality; Simon had to leave his role as guide. After about a year there was a clear change when he confided his life-story to me. That was a moment of intense religious experience.

Although at that time we thought that expressions of sexuality had to have limits, ours was certainly an affective relationship. When we met more often, our friendship took on more shape. I was then living in a group with sisters who knew about our friendship and encouraged me in it. This very experience of a fine friendship seemed to have given my contacts with others understanding, warmth and passion.

After about three years I had a crisis as a result of a change of work, study and abode. I got the feeling of having been left in the lurch by everyone, including Simon. He was more accustomed than I was to keeping our friendship secret from those around. That I lived with others was a reason for him no longer to come to visit me. But that didn't seem to be the only one. After one of the few times we saw each other and went into town in a friendly way, the word got out: he had begun a relationship with another woman just as I was finding things really difficult. But he didn't want to break off the relationship with me, since we meant so much to each other.

I was utterly bowled over by this report and asked myself what I meant to him and how he could divide his attention like this? Was his other friend sometimes more on his "level"? Because at this time I felt very alone and couldn't do without our friendship, I resolved to agree to his proposal, and I even told him that I thought it desirable that his love and attention should go not only to me but to also to someone else. That was the start of a kind of wave of crises in our relationship. During the next fifteen years

Simon shared his attention and love with two and later three women friends.

When we were together we sensed a great bond. For me that feeling of a bond also continued when he went away. But I often came to the painful conclusion that this was not the case with him. Sometimes he was away or I couldn't reach him, or for a long time I heard nothing from him.

Despite this other relationship, my friendship with Simon continued and slowly took firmer shape. We agreed to meet for a weekend a month. Only a meeting of the order or the congregation was to be a reason for deviating from this. In the meantime we had both come to live alone, and on the days we spent together it was great to have each other's company. We could share the good moments and the difficult moments of the time that had gone past, the excitement at what we had experienced, the pain and the disappointment at what went wrong or didn't succeed in our small world of work, family and others who were dear to us or crossed our paths. We were also particularly interested in developments in the church and society and also in the Third World. Because of his job Simon was often more involved with church matters, while I was more in the thick of society. In this way we supplemented each other well and we valued this in each other a lot. We went for walks along the sea shore, in the woods or other country spots. The peace and quiet and the feeling of each other's presence meant that we had some unforgettably fine moments. In addition, good films and modern art had a special attraction for Simon, and over the course of years I also began to see this and value it. We tried to enjoy things together to discover the meaning of modern life in them. We also pursued the religious symbolism surrounding love, life and death.

We had breakfast on Sunday morning as a festive beginning to the week, quiet, with music and Holy Scripture and a good conversation. Sometimes we went to a eucharist on Sunday or we tried to express the weekend we were spending together by spontaneous prayers or meditative texts. We often celebrated the breaking and sharing of our life together or with others whom we had invited. During these meetings we grew increasingly familiar with each other. We also became so familiar with each other's bodies in our expressions of tenderness and love that a complete sexual relationship was natural. We found so much good and attractiveness in it that we both had the feeling that it couldn't be wrong. I've never had guilt feelings about it. On the contrary, I've found friendship liberating and become another person as a result. The affective, sexual side of it made me blossom as a woman into gentleness, understanding and passion. Even in the pain and sorrow of breaking off the relationship I had an experience which, however painful, gave me the chance to stand closer in my work to people who had to work through similar experiences.

In later years we both went on holiday together. Not too often or too long, since Simon wanted to keep our relationship secret from the people he met in his work.

My family was well aware of the situation, and shortly before she died, after we had visited her together, my mother said, "How splendid that you love each other so much." Simon was very close to me during the illnesses and deaths of my parents. He also came to both their funerals. That made a strong bond and at the same time caused some pain because I was so little involved with his family. There was the same difference in contact with others. Here I constantly felt more free about our relationship, and he had more difficulty with it. In retrospect, I think that this wasn't just because as a priest he couldn't show himself with a woman, because I noticed that he sometimes took other women friends to his family and relations.

There were periods when we came very close to each other in our friendship. At other moments we felt that our bond was less strong and I sometimes had the feeling that we were driving each other away. Then the sense of intimacy became more difficult for me, above all when Simon was unattainable, both literally and in giving his attention. That was when he had a visit from his other woman friend, was working somewhere with her or had gone on holiday with her. At those moments I was evidently unimportant. For example, I once telephoned him because I felt very sick and alone. I was afraid that I had some serious ailment and had no one else to talk to. But although he lived nearby he didn't come, because he had his other women friend visiting. So I had to ask one of the neighbours to take me to the hospital late at night. At that moment I really felt left in the lurch.

Often I had the feeling that I was being kept out of his life. Thus he celebrated the anniversaries of his profession and his ordination with his closest friends, but I was not one of them. Nevertheless he assured me that he had the most intimate relationship with me. And I had to be the one who could understand why he couldn't invite two women friends to a party. He kept his women friends, his anniversaries and such occasions well apart, and was always busy revolving round them. He didn't make a clear choice and under the mantle of "being there for many" he had his mollycoddling everywhere and was always "under cover". He not only expected me to understand and regard as normal the fact that he had more relationships, but also encouraged me to have other relationships. I did fall in love a couple of times, but it never got as far as a relationship. For me it's impossible to maintain several deep relationships at the same time.

However, when I once fell for one of Simon's colleagues, Simon was quite upset by it, although I didn't plan to enter into a serious relationship. It seemed as if I was his possession. "If it had been anyone else, but this!" It was impossible, I had to understand that a friend of his was involved here. During a course and a study trip in which all three of us took part, I was as it were watched by Simon. Even my looks were observed.

The difficulties between us increased when I discovered by chance that for a year Simon had already had a third woman friend. My amazement and fury at so much unfairness was overwhelming. He seemed to have different standards for himself which didn't apply to me.

Meanwhile Simon had gone into therapy. There he had discovered that he had lacked love in his youth. As a result he was now so greedy and so happy and pleased when someone loved him that he immediately surrendered to this love. He gave a rational explanation for his behaviour but didn't change it in any way. It was as though he couldn't do anything about it, as though it was that of someone else. But I started to talk to him again and he promised to drop the relationship with his last women friend, who he said was neurotic and made claims on him. Although I slowly got the feeling that irrevocable things had happened, we continued to meet each other now and then. During one of these

99

meetings he told me that at the weekend he had had a visit from woman friend number three. Instead of being dropped, the relationship had just intensified. That was the limit.

It was then that I sought help. And once I had let all my bottled-up feelings of disappointment, hurt and anger come out, it became clear to me that I had to make a choice. I sensed that Simon had not really let me share his life and that I was one of a series for him. I had now lost my last remnant of trust in him, and even if he gave up the other relations for me, he had gone too far.

My own role in the process has also become clearer to me. I didn't draw clear limits. I had concern and compassion for him when he was a leader. I felt responsible to him and sometimes turned my crossness and anger against myself for fear of losing him. After two conversations with a counsellor I resolved that I would no longer be possessed either by him or by my own anxieties or by feeling responsible for him. Simon, shocked by my resolve, asked me to postpone the decision and to give him a few months to sort himself out. However, he said that I mustn't count on his giving up his other relationships. What was I to do? Go on waiting, wait and wait again? No, by then I had had enough, and I drew a firm line under a relationship which had lasted twenty years. That was a great step for me, and I still can't see all the consequences. It almost seemed as if it were untrue, as if it couldn't be true, and I noticed that I left him bewildered.

Going on alone

To begin with I was very tired and tense. I found it very difficult to accept that it was really over. Precisely because I was alone with it, it was difficult for me to grasp the reality, and I constantly had the feeling that it couldn't be true. When the reality did get through, the pain, the sorrow and the disappointment came, while many things in my home reminded me of the happy hours that I had spent with Simon. Then anger and hurt came on top of a feeling of emptiness and loss. I had to sort out all these feelings by myself, because it was difficult to discuss them with others. What prevented me from being open over them?

First was the fact that many people in my circle of acquaintances hadn't known of the relationship or at any rate of its content, the real love, the religious dimension and its great significance in my life. I was just afraid that they wouldn't understand.

Secondly, I was afraid that there would be disapproval, implied or expressed, about the physical, even sexual, side of our relationship, which would lead to denial of the other dimensions of our friendship.

Moreover I didn't want to bring Simon into discredit. Did I still care for his good name and want to protect him? I also discovered that our relationship really had the character of a "*romance à deux*", a world of experience which we had shared together and which had not been accessible to others. Another consequence of this was that I largely had to undergo and work out my process of mourning by myself.

At this time I saw Simon just once more and talked with him. The aim of this meeting was to share with each other how to cope with the parting. On this occasion Simon suggested that we should go and see a film together, because we had enjoyed that so much in the past. He saw no possibilities of further contact. This proposal only made me cross; it made me feel used. Of course I didn't agree, but chose to go to the film alone. The first film I saw without Simon was the one based on Kundera's *The Incredible Lightness of Being*. For me it was quite incomprehensible how unsympathetic Simon was to my feelings. I felt he had not done me justice, whether during our friendship, at our parting, or in the way in which making and breaking off contact was now being done.

Of course that was also true of his contacts with others. He once told me that his other woman friend(s) made the same complaint. He used this information as a kind of excuse, rather like "You see I spread my attention equally over you all."

Meanwhile I began to miss a relationship very much. My life seemed to become flat and empty, as if it had lost meaning and significance. Sometimes quite ordinary things took on significance by being shared, by the feeling of loving him and being loved by him. It gave colour to life which had previously been colourless. Now I notice that I no longer find many things worthwhile. I used to take photographs of nature, and now it seems to do nothing for me. Sometimes I feel involved in the congregation, but at other times I find little involvement or real contact.

I turn to silence and reflection, and really feel the emptiness and the loss in that. I hope to draw courage and energy from it to see more future.

About a year ago I sometimes had the inclination, because of my anxiety about being alone, to go back on my concern for something new and the advice of others, to begin the relationship with Simon all over again. But then I really would have been denying myself. Now I'm further on with my process. Above all by writing my story I've become clearer about how things were and what problems there were in our relationship.

I now know for certain that I shall go on without Simon, without the great moments but also without always sharing someone's pain and sorrow with others. I'm all too well aware that I didn't do justice either to myself or to his other women friends. If Simon wants to console himself with the thought that in this way he meant much to several people, he should also know that it caused them pain, sorrow, disappointment and loneliness.

I allowed this story to be published beause I suspect that in the circles of women religious there are more women who have had to share their "priest friend" with someone else in a comparable way. Those among them who find this a problem may possibly find insight here and a way of dealing with it.'

Annemaria

Living is to be loved
To become truth
Be without end
Love is living round being.

He was thirty-six and she was eighteen when they got to know each other. He was a priest of the Sacred Heart; she was studying at the social academy. Their friendship began, as so many do, in a work situation.

Vincent and she fell in love with each other. 'We kept it a secret for three or four years.' It was in 1965, and in many areas of society processes of renewal were beginning. 'Anyone could see that we were in love with each other. But,' she said with a laugh, 'we did very ordinary things.' Then Vincent was suddenly moved. He was to become a chaplain in H. But he deliberately failed the test for it. Nor did he settle in R. It became a final decision. He left the order and began to look for a place. From A he went to a small vilage in Drenthe. How do you arrive at such a decision? I asked her whether he came out in order to be able to marry. 'Everyone asks that, but I can't give an answer. The two things are connected. I wouldn't like it if he had come out only for me. It grew like that; they suspected that we were in love with each other. We didn't like the fact that he was to be moved. Then he had to put a stop to it. My parents sent me to France to think things over.'

On arriving in his new home and place of work in Drenthe he asked her father if they could marry. Father didn't have much difficulty with this, but other members of the family raised all kinds of objections and claimed that priests of that age had already 'played around' with so many women. That was then. Later they were very positive about them both. 'He was too old; I was still only twenty-one and moreover he was a priest. His family, who were staunch Catholics, had to take a great deal.' Finally Vincent brought her from Paris. She went to live in the same village, but in a different house. You didn't sleep together at that time. During the day they were together.

Later they married, in the chapel of his priory. It was a very good service. Her family were there, but of his family only his youngest brother. 'His mother just telephoned secretly.' Of course she couldn't accept the marriage of her former priest son. It was a shock to the staunch Catholic family, which consisted of parents and sixteen children.

Vincent and she hoped for children. She had a miscarriage and then a stillborn child. 'That's the result,' people said. Later three children were born from their marriage.

'To begin with I noticed that he had quite a different life history from mine. After the birth of our first child he saw how much care a child needed; before that he had never stopped to think about it. As a priest you were to some degree detached from the actual world of "ordinary" people.'

They were very different. She noticed that herself, and other people also said that to them. As an example she mentioned the arrangement of their home. 'He told me that that sort of thing wasn't important. "It's only a means," he said then.'

Although he was twice as old as she was when they got to know each other, because of his sheltered upbringing he had far less experience of life. The love was boundless; the loving had to be learned. 'Later it was violent.' There was emotion in her voice when she said, 'Vincent loved me very much; you could see that, everyone could see it.'

When their oldest child was born, he cried out, 'It's alive', and he was utterly overwhelmed that this could happen, having a child. He was unlike other fathers. Younger men are often still occupied with their careers: he always had lots of concern for the children. The oldest child was eleven when Vincent fell sick. He grew thin and began to worry about his health, but it was a long time before he went to a doctor. When he became really ill, I said, "You knew it all along, didn't you?" He confirmed this: for a long time he had had the feeling of being incurably ill. But he didn't want to leave his family. He sometimes talked about death. "When I'm dead, you must say that while I had a short life, it was an intense one." He wasn't afraid of dying, because he wasn't afraid of living. "You must dare to be authentic," he often said.'

The doctor found nothing in his examination. The consultant said, 'At most a very small swelling.' He had an operation. Then it proved that nothing else could be done. The cancer was in an advanced stage. Annemaria brought him home, against the advice of the doctors, to die. They had two weeks to say goodbye. He died in her arms; the children were also there.

'Up to the last moment he didn't act as if he were ill. Everything had to go on as usual. Despite everything, it was a very good time in our life. You were completely thrown back on yourself, all masks removed. You began to see the essential things, to be really yourself.' In the hospital he was cared for by a good friend. This priest also took the funeral. 'It was in the church of the Red Dean of Limburg. It was moving, a splendid service.'

Then came the loneliness. She visited all the places where Vincent had ever lived, including his old lodgings. She had a photograph but didn't know the address and asked people in the village. 'O,' said a man, 'that is Catharina de Liefde, whose funeral is taking place this very moment.' At that moment the church bell began to toll, a sign of someone's burial. For her it was a sign to let the past rest and look to the future. 'Vincent always said, "Don't get buried in the past." That was a sign for me. He also often said that you must always use your understanding and then colour it with your feeling. He always worked, day and night, and I didn't like that very much. Probably guilt-feelings, because he had come out, and as a result of his education. He had a very strict discipline for himself. Anything that didn't finish you off made you stronger. Over the past two years I've grown ten years older. Earlier I noticed that I looked younger than I was, but now my face matches my age. I used to be the little girl. He was the one who said how things should be. I didn't mind this; I was used to it at home: Papa had the say. My mother also thought that this was all right. It's really very easy when you have no responsibility.'

After her husband's death, there was a great transition. She had to learn to be independent. 'But step by step it worked.'

Vincent was not her first man. She had had another friend. To begin with, Vincent was a colleague, then he became an older friend. They felt attracted to each other, went to the cinema together. 'We saw all the Bergman films together. We could meet in the dark.'

In this love story it is not Eve who leads Adam astray with an apple. 'He always used to take an apple to work. One day he peeled the apple and gave me a piece, went very red, a blush. He told me that he loved me. Then we also exchanged our first kisses after a year of secret feelings for each other. During the marriage the parents on both sides became reconciled to us. It was fine, great children, a good marriage. Vincent didn't miss his priesthood. He still regularly took part in ecumenical services. He could put his heart into training. He was good at many things. Nor was his priesthood directed outside. It was in him. He was a balanced person. A whole person.' She enthusiastically told how he shared in household tasks. 'He could string beans for a whole afternoon. Sang the Ave Maria under the shower. His first concern was always whether all was well with the children. Really I'm only getting to know him now. I think so often, "So that's what he meant." '

Was she against the church? 'No, they know no more than I do. The pope knows more than I do. I have a love in heaven. The pope doesn't have that, or he's lying. Vincent also saw the crazy things about the church. He fundamentally disagreed with the institutional church. He thought that it was criminal when it prevented people from thinking and kept them inmmature. That went against his whole understanding. He wanted people to think for themselves and act on that basis. He thought people's own responsibility very important.

I think that his training as a priest contributed strongly to his being such a perceptive person. He penetrated all mere appearances. It was as if he always remained out of range, but there was also nothing remarkable about him. He was a tremendous partner, a marvellous father. He made me see the essentials of life.'

Who are the women?

I was a premature child and spent the first two months of my life in hospital. Possibly because of that I had no relationship with my mother and my feminine side and I rejected her, everything feminine, and the feminine in myself. I had a great father. He was integrated, caring, strong and playful, and I became what they call 'daddy's daughter'. With him I felt safe and secure. He was a man of few words and I was also a silent child. We had an almost telepathic contact and understood each other at a glance. Only much later did I learn that precisely as a result of this silence there was no differentiation, and that in identifying with him I remained the little girl.

Like my father, I had a strong inner world of experience, which in the almost mediaeval climate, the village sphere, in which I lived, was fed above all by the church, the ceremonies and the sacred. I took in and integrated images of God as the good father and providential governor of heaven and earth. Only later, when I became aware of the *animus*, did I sense that my father-image, my image of God and my image of the male aroused the same feelings of emotion, warmth and security.

In one phase of my youth, at a junior school run by nuns, the heretic awoke in me, a sub-personality which was instilled by my mother, who was definitely not pious and astute. This heretic still lived a repressed life because she didn't feel able to cope with the sexless beings hidden in black habits who tried to make me a good girl. I've never been that good girl at heart, but through the pressure of circumstances I allowed myself to be seduced into playing such a role. Being good and nice, interested and enchanted, asking nothing for myself and everything for others.

So two worlds took shape in me: a female/male side and a male/female side.

In my adolescence these two sides seem to have taken separate profiles. The female side wanted to go into the world, away from the sphere of a bourgeois village; sought freedom without any need for family life or motherhood. My mother always supported me in this, and later I understood how much she had also wanted such a life for herself. She was a feminist at heart, intelligent, fond of travelling and social, but tied to her limited milieu of that time and place. My other, male, side turned inwards and began to translate the erotic need that I certainly had into 'mystical' experiences. The search for that occupied me a long time. I didn't dare talk about it. I had no words for it, wasn't affirmed in it, because it was tabu at that time and in the church to talk of experiences. Later it became clear to me that latent eroticism also plays a role in mediaeval mysticism of love, which nevertheless must find a landing place somewhere. And it has also become clear to me that these experiences had a very stimulating influence on my dedication in life, but that it was a still immature experience of God, to be compared with the difference between being in love and love. Through all this, God was my partner in life and I his servant, whose task was to serve him and to proclaim his love in the world. I really wanted to be a man, become a priest. But how could you realize that as a woman? In a convent? Never!

I chose the way of a less strict secular institution which was more in the world, with a normal position in society. It was a function in the soft sector, where I was confronted with quite different sides of life from those I had known at home and with the harsh reality in which many people have to live. For me that meant a considerable degree of awareness and the development of a feminine eye for situations and facts. At this time I mostly had no need of a man; I couldn't possibly see a family and children as an ideal (at that time that was part of sexual experience) and I was little aware of my body and its longings. Moreover I was looking for a man who was 'stronger' than I, and where could I find this but in my father or in God? This is perhaps the reason why I never wanted to form a tie to friends or men whom I met. Fortunately the contacts I have had in this respect left their traces: little steps towards a sense of feminity.

Something remained in me which sought 'the one authentic thing' in relations with men. The one authentic person came into view when I was thirty-three, in a working group with Father X. In him I found the one whom I had unconsciously sought all my life. He corresponded to my ideal picture, and I could identify with him. I fell head over heels in love with him.

I was happy in my relationship with him and fortunate in his care. I was proud to be able to have such an inspired personality as a partner, felt chosen because out of so many admirers he had picked me for himself. My feminine side developed and grew. I seemed to have unexpected gentle yet strong qualities; in short I became another person and more of a person. On his side he proved to be a grateful recipient of all that I had to offer him and gave him.

At the spiritual level we had long been rooted in an impossible life of faith which offered much warmth and security but which – however ecumenically – was protected from the real world. We found each other in this church, and we looked in it for awareness and emancipation. He sought this above all within the church structure. For me, however, the heretic soon emerged and I detached myself from the secular institute, theological training and the church. As a result my world narrowed. I began to cling more to his person and made myself a spouse.

I idealized our intimate relationship. I thought that we were getting on very well. Apparently everything was possible and we were very free towards each other, though sexual intercourse seldom occurred. When I asked for it more at a later stage, he refused and said that I mustn't ask for more. Now I feel that there was no equality and no real 'union'. When I raised questions about the relationship he replied with a pastoral or spiritual answer, which put the question on to another, 'higher' plane. At the level of intimacy I functioned as a servant, who was at his every bidding. I was also the caring mother at moments when he really became the small boy, which I shuddered at in my heart. But perhaps that's also a caricature. There was another side. That of ordinary everyday life with an ordinary man. For in my conscious life I saw him as a partner in life who could be very companionable, who was grateful for small pieces of attention, full of humour, with whom I talked endlessly and with whom I went for walks. But his other side remained full of an ideal picture for which he had to do heroic deeds, for which he had to be holy, and for which past life was of little value. I think that I gave the ordinary person too few chances because I seemed to glorify him and stood up too little for the woman in myself, whom he really loved, to whom he paid compliments about her looks and dress. This ordinary man and this ordinary woman got on very well, felt equal and grew together in their experiences. I still find it sad that they didn't succeed together. I find the pain of this failure more difficult to bear than the pain of growing awareness, because this ultimately had more positive sides.

Growing awareness. The real change in me began when we were apart for the first time for a couple of years. I began as it were to work on myself and as a result got to know another man. In contact with him my eyes and my heart were opened. He radiated a different male image, had a more relaxed and recognized need for the physical, a quest for spirituality rooted in reality, and took equality much more for granted. He was also more critical about me as a woman. 'You put far too high demands on a man, demands which no normal person can fulfil.' A relationship with this man, who had his ties, was neither possible nor necessary, but through him I got to know my *animus* and felt the need to integrate it. It was very strong, but gradually came under control, also because my feminine side was still not developed completely and because my partner had simply referred to particular facets of it. In this new contact qualities were brought out in me which I recognized and acknowledged gratefully. He accepted the lover, the wise woman and also the critical conceited witch – whom my partner had feared – as though they were the most natural thing in the world. Thus armed, I again – at his request – entered into relations with my former friend. We hadn't shared so many years for nothing, and we were, it seemed, still familiar with each other. In the meantime my friend had also undergone a development. He proved freer and dared to show his need for intimacy more. A hopeful new beginning, but the new relationship raised a number of problems. Without our becoming aware of it we fell back into old patterns. I couldn't find any form in which my now changed personality could have peace and he simply didn't understood why I worried about it. Only now do I see, after the questionnaire and all that it released in me, that the problem really lurked in the church and faith. For me these had completely disappeared from view, but for him they still seemed fed by the old pattern, hidden behind another social and spiritual attitude.

First of all he would not acknowledge, either to his friends and acquaintances or to the church and his order, what to my thinking was an authentic relationship. He wanted to remain a priest in the eyes of the world. Secondly, he still had hidden guilt-feelings about sexuality, which expressed themselves in a desire to make love 'spiritually'. As long as it had a spiritual name and purpose, anything was clearly possible. And then to take out these spiritual feelings on me! No wonder that I felt violated, or the unpaid whore. It was not a matter of me and our relationship; it was a matter of using me for his 'spiritual' experiments. Please understand. I think that making love can develop into a cosmic experience, but you can't intend, plan that, just as you cannot and may not force spiritual experiences. And again in the first instance I suppressed the heretic in me because I simply didn't want to believe that a deity could intend anything like this and I dared not make this deity angry. Fortunately, this anger came later, when I began to take my feelings seriously. But when I did that, he put all the responsibility on me, as though it was not something that we did together.

I now regard my anger as a further development of my woman-hood and of accepting the heretic or the witch in me. To be honest, I have to say that my own purposes in beginning the relationship again were not completely unimportant. I wanted to fulfil the needs that had been aroused in me with a real lover, and rightly so. But at least I gave them a name which accorded with reality. If we had had the roles of ordinary man and woman, perhaps all would have gone well. But I refused to have the label of 'spirituality' put on normal physical needs. I took both spirituality and those needs too seriously for that.

But I was confronted with my not being able to be angry with the priest in him. In this respect did I still see him as a kind of saint? And don't many women who are 'in love' with a priest look at things like this, even if not in a relationship? In recent weeks I've thought back to that and observed that I'm again angry with the church which causes this. This anger expresses itself in the following thoughts.

'The male side of some women is developed by a priest. Unfortunately not the reality of this priest, but the ideal picture. The reality of priests, certainly of those with these semi-sexual relations, is that as a result of their training and their position in church and society they are often not in a position to enter into normal relations, certainly not with women. What they can do generally is to appear as a father (confessor) as long as they find enough young girls who admire them as such, love them, cherish them in their hearts, in short, with whom they can play the father. Like a deity on a throne, sexless and invulnerable. Many women find a certain satisfaction in worshipping such a deity or idol.

In addition, the same priests can sometimes also easily adopt the role of child and seek security with a mother (the church) which cherishes them, looks after them and pampers them, to whom they can cry and even shout about the dangers of the big evil world in which they have been forced to play the role of strong, omnipotent and omniscient figures. Many women are all too ready to show their maternal feelings to these priests, above all if they themselves have no children.

These priests are not in a position to have a relationship on an equal footing; they've never learned that. They find it difficult to find a middle way between their own high ideals and the small boy, or better, they cannot find themselves, their adult selves.'

I'm very aware that for a long time I've been the little girl in relation to my partner. I've certainly also played the mother figure, by beginning to feel responsible, among other things, for his spiritual development and independence. These two things go together. For the small girl who spiritually dares not stand on her own feet looks for a father to support her, not in her identity but in her role as the little girl. The mother figure then becomes all too concerned, not for the real identity of the other, but for the role of the little boy. These two poles apparently keep each other in balance, but that balance is false. There is a balance in an equality which is based on each other's own identity. We haven't been able to find this balance in our relationship. At the same time I sense that it is the heretic/witch in me which is driving me to this and that I have/had the choice between remaining the little girl and growing up. With pain in my heart, I've opted for the latter and feel happy about it, because as a result I've produced and still produce something authentic in my life.

In my view spiirtuality has everything to do with becoming a self who is not only confessed on the lips but also perceived in everyday reality, since spirituality has everything to do with perceiving that that self is present in every other person, even if it is concealed.

Priests, the vow to celibacy and intimate relations

How does it come about that there are priests who begin to see their vow of celibacy as something that was perhaps right earlier, but now takes on quite a different content for them? Do they simply break it, as being out-of-date? Or do other factors determine entering into a relationship which is forbidden by the church? In the questionnaire a question about this was put to the women of priests. In their answers they indicated how they felt their partner thought about the church. Doubtless there will be differences between the interpretation of the women and the ideas of the men as they expressed them. During the meetings I organized it emerged that the priests hardly ever talked to colleagues about their relationship. They didn't mention it or denied it to their women. It is well known that men talk less about their relationship than women. Moreover, it is a threat for priests to talk about their women friends; they can lose their job if it becomes known that they have an intimate relationship with a woman. But a problem which emerges so often deserves attention. Or has everyone found his own private solution?

Some priests were prepared to say something. These are stories of people who have undergone growth and deliberately made a choice, people who now have a happy relationship. So they form one particular group. The other groups, priests who maintain several relationships at the same time, priests who have children or suddenly break off their relationship without talking plainly with their women, remained silent. No story could be got from them – because their ex-women friends maintained their anonymity, or had no intention of asking them. In one case questions were asked but the priest would say no more. Perhaps his story was too difficult to tell; perhaps the silence indicated shame or there was a total denial.

A priest looks back

There are priests who have undergone a change in their lives, have begun to see women with other eyes, have adopted other values and norms, especially over friendship and love. One of them looks back.

'It can be said so clearly: I shall write it down. But now it's there before me I feel like a mountain climber who would prefer to say, "I'm looking up, but I'm not climbing this mountain." We shall see how far we get. First something about my background in the sphere of relationships.

In my student days women and sex were a dangerous area. It was the time when periodic abstinence for married people was accepted reluctantly. We students thought that these were things which married people had to work out for themselves. We felt that it was none of our business. At that time sexuality was already taking on more of a positive ring as an expression of love. For me there was never any real doubt whether I should become a priest, and I sensed that you had to take that way alone. However, I found women and girls very attractive. I was to become a priest, and celibacy was regarded as an obstacle on the way to priesthood. At that time the idea that as a priest you could marry never occurred to me. It was clear; marriage and priesthood could not be combined. I worked enthusiastically as a priest in different parishes. I was happy. I felt at home in my work and with people. I lived in my liturgical celebrations. I was fond of people. I got completely involved in all the changes which were taking place at that time. During those years friendships with married couples grew. You entered freely into friendship with one another, and also with women friends. So I came to the frontiers of eroticism. I now realize that I was never completely happy here. However, the greater openness was very attractive. It was the time when I discovered how great it was to have a woman friend, and yet there was also an element of stealing. But it was safe: unmarried friends would have made other demands.

Married friends already had a life with tasks and family concerns. I could come and go with them.

This is a time on which I look back with not undivided pleasure. At that time I came to know my present woman friend. We've now been together for years. The beginning was difficult. I was used to pushing aside many things, hiding my emotions. She was open and radical. She soon discovered something of that world in me. I tried to compromise, with her and her other women friends: was it very different, my relationship with her and my relationship with others? Did it have to develop? I told her everything honestly, and even as I told her it became clear to me that things couldn't go on like that. I had to choose, and I have chosen.

It was often very difficult to be open, to make myself known. I could no longer shut things off, not only from her but also from myself. That's a big process of change, for which much courage was needed. There was also a third openness: being open to the outside world. From the very beginning we didn't keep our relationship secret. We did everything together to the outside world. We have many things in common. I also find that a firm cement for our friendly relationship. It's a marvellous feeling to be able to be open and free wherever you are. We live together in a presbytery and I do my pastoral work as a priest; she does her own work.

I feel rich in my love. I've become much more of a "person". My feelings have become richer and deeper, my body has increasingly become my home. I've learned to listen to it. It's so much less inhibited. I continue to learn, especially to put into words what is happening to me. My friend is my best teacher here. I have the feeling that I'm now really at home with her and with myself. Earlier I was in transit; I came and went between friendly couples. Deep in my heart I knew that I didn't belong in that sort of thing. But for a while I had to silence this voice, because I didn't want to lose it. Perhaps it's been a training school for someone who still has to get to know his own feelings. Now I talk about human relations in a different way. I feel their riches and discover how difficult it is to find an answer to the question, "Who are you to me, who am I to you?"

But to be able to go on like this makes me feel a king. A real blessing!'

Getting out

Ralph and Joanna fell in love with one another, as happens between a man and a woman. There was one problem: Ralph was a priest. Was, for he's no longer a priest – though you're a priest for ever. He has found another kind of work in which he's just as committed to the life of others, more closely concerned for daily existence. He was fortunate; he found a new career. What form did that process of falling in love and deciding to come out take? Such a story isn't easy to tell. Ralph and Joanna tried.

How did you get to know each other? What happened to you?

Ralph: 'In 1985 I had organized an ecumenical youth trip to East Germany with some colleagues, a cultural and religious programme. The first day of the journey I got to know Joanna. In the bus I was attracted by a face that said a lot to me. Up until that moment I was definitely not in search of a friendship or relationship with a woman. I had only been two years in K, to set up a new youth chaplaincy, and was full of enthusiasm about it. I was "invited" after a sabbatical year in F, where I had been able to learn some inspiring initiatives. I had a full schedule in K, worked sixty hours a week, no attention to myself, no listening to my own doubts, uncertanities, needs. The deeper questions of the sabbatical year were snowed under: who am I without a ministry around me, as a naked believer? Where do I stand, where do I feel safe, how to I cope with loneliness, with sexuality? It was as if the encounter with Joanna confronted me with this repressed side of myself. Without my wanting it, a world of erotic feelings opened up: a longing to feel warm, to feel close to each other. I found it very threatening that a girl began to love me, because that was not what I sought. I was certainly very attracted. It hurt me and at the same time I found it good.

In the week on vacation in East Germany everything was turned upside down. I had already had many women friends and had not been brought up prudishly, but I had constantly hidden myself. Now I suddenly burned fiercely with desire.

During that year Joanna had to do part-time practical work with me in the youth chaplaincy. There was a double agenda; it was marvellous that someone was also concerned for me as a person. I tried to meet Joanna twice a week. For discussions of work, but also privately. A new warm stream came into my life. It was all so new, I couldn't yet give it a place. Was she perhaps just one of the points on my agenda, to which I was wedded? I could only talk with a couple of friends about my feelings and experiences. What I enjoyed about Joanna was her warmth, her inwardness, her spirituality, her choices, her view of life. Sexually I felt very attracted to her. From the side of the church, the obligation to celibacy and the like, I felt few inhibitions. It was as if a natural voice was saying to me: just dare to be yourself, to take down your barriers. Do you feel that this contact is a liberation? Of course there was a conflict. I couldn't reconcile my longings with the expectations associated with my office. But I wasn't afraid, I didn't run away, but thought: "Just let it happen, it'll turn out well." Moreover I was very careful with Joanna and this experience. She was twenty and I was forty-one. So I had no illusions, though I hardly felt that this difference in age was an obstacle.'

Joanna: 'After some short, unsatisfactory contacts with boy friends I had had enough of men. My life was focussed on a few good friends, men and women, and I didn't need more. The encounter with Ralph was therefore one of doubt: am I entering into something that makes no sense? Ralph overwhelmed me when it became clear that he was head over heels in love. I was also in love, but thought that it would be temporary. We were both amazed about it. For after a year it proved that we could say to each other that we wanted to go on together. I had grown up in a short time. I wanted to experience the consequences which followed from this relationship. We bore a great responsibility for each other. Up to that point I had lived for this alone. That puts other demands on you.

This relationship has to be good. You make such a venture only once. We've talked a lot and marked out stages. That happens at the expense of relaxation and enjoying each other.

Ralph sometimes says that I keep him young, and through him I've grown up. The difference in age is no longer such a great gap.'

It is claimed that women are 'seduced' by priests. Which of you took the first step?

Ralph: 'I think that I took the first step. I gave clear signals. Joanna reacted, I think, in amazement. Curious, but also very careful. Not rejecting or closed. But let her speak for herself...'

Joanna: 'When I went on the trip I knew that I would be going with Ralph. I noticed that he had a more than usual interest in me. My first reaction was anxiety. Was I the umpteenth girl friend? And surely that was wrong for priests? Why did he find me so attractive? I waited. But Ralph also became my friend. In East Germany we always sat next to each other in the bus. We got a chance to know each other better. In a work situation that would have taken longer. It was the beginning of really falling in love. But also of anxiety at the unknown.'

You had fallen in love. You were both aware of that. At what stage of your love did sex begin to play a role?

Ralph: 'I needed us to share each other's warmth completely. I think that that feeling, the certainty that it was good, also had something to do with my age. We saw each other often.'

Joanna: 'After a couple of months we could go away for a weekend and for the first time spent two nights together. When I think back on this beginning period I see that we fumbled a lot.'

Did faith, the church and the church's decisions come into play at an early stage?

Ralph: 'I'm a Catholic, Joanna was originally Reformed. In our thought and conviction we moved into a sphere where we began to feel at home, into the critical open society in which commitment exists and a spirituality of resistance. At all events I felt strongly responsible for myself and my own conscience. We talked about this. Of course Joanna also knew of the priest's obligation to celibacy. But she understood very well how I personally felt.'

Joanna answers from her background. In the Protestant world the minister is one among equals. In the Catholic world the priest stands above the laity.

Joanna: 'My Protestant background gave me a more matter-of-fact view of all these Catholic matters. Because everything was new for me I could put critical questions. Dismay and amazement. We talked a lot about the Catholic tradition. I noticed that Ralph took an independent position on it. He was certainly a child of his time, a child of his upbringing. But he didn't accept it all unreservedly. In this sense he had a free upbringing. As a result, for me the church remained more in the background.'

Joanna, can you say what you felt for Ralph?

Joanna: 'In the first instance he was not the "man of my dreams". I overcame some resistance in myself before I chose Ralph. It was clear that such a relationship is intense and demanding and can only happen once. If our relationship had gone wrong, I don't know whether I would have had the courage to enter into another one.'

Ralph, you made a promise to the church, in the face of God, as the church puts it. How do you interpret that now? For you is it just a revision of celibacy, or is it also a reorientation on faith?'

Ralph: 'I always loved the church, and gave myself to it heart and soul. And I've received a good deal from it. I might put it like this: I was very popular with young people, I was very much loved in the parish: in living liturgy in which there could be laughter but also in the crisis pastorate (divorces, caring for the dying). I stood in this church. But I was afraid that I would have to become one of those ultimately responsible in a church which was also powerful, yet as an institution was remote from the reality of younger people. I didn't want to become a piece of furniture in the same parish; I wanted to grow, to get to know more about the dynamic church, to look over barriers. That also applied to my own life.

I also see my promise to the church along these lines. I never saw it as a strict legal promise. My ordination as priest had already cost me a great deal. At this time I had parted from a girl friend (though I had not had sexual intercourse with her). This step had cost me a lot and the church was dear to me. But in this church I wasn't known as a person, but simply as an inspiring workhorse, as a driving force, and that began to take its toll. Moreover I constantly told young people that faithfulness and the power to grow isn't a legal agreement, that it's always a matter of being true to yourself, continually listening to your deepest feelings. I could talk so splendidly to other people and go along with them here. I myself had to accept guidance like a blind man, from someone much younger who with warmth and directness asked me to be ordinary Ralph. I didn't see my growing relationship with Joanna as a break with the church. A deeper trust developed in me, in what I had constantly suppressed in myself through slavery to pastoral work (it was sin, it was an attack on my health – spiritually as well – it mocked nature and was thus against God's purposes). It led to reflection on the significance of my monastic vows. I reached the stage of thinking that breaking these vows needn't amount to being unfaithful to myself or to God or to the church. I felt that I was constantly becoming more whole, and also began to see how I had constantly eluded myself. My life of faith began to change a lot through this experience. I became less the minister and more the believer. A move began to take place from the inspiring president to the seeking believer. Slowly but surely I came round to the other side of the counter. Human experiences with the church (pain, rebellion, wrestling) also became my own story.'

Will you and can you say anything about your feelings after the first time that you had gone to bed together, became "man and wife"? Was there any experience of a creative happening? Was it related to your faith?

Ralph: 'I can still remember it well. It was a really explosive event, like a hurricane, the fulfilling of a long desire. I wanted to give myself wholly to Joanna. For me she was the revelation for which I had waited so long. To my mind it had nothing to do with my belief. Nor did I experience anything creative in it. I do recall that we had grown into it. It was very exciting, like a teenager discovering intimacy. It gave me the feeling that I never wanted to live without Joanna. Also, it was something so irrevocable for me that I couldn't and wouldn't give myself to anyone else. In retrospect the whole love play was very short; I didn't yet know any emotional basis. I was a child and had so much to learn.'

Joanna: 'No, not a creative event or a story of faith. Nor a romantic "first time". We were so taken up with going to bed together that our emotion for each other was secondary. It was there, certainly, even very strongly there. But it was as if we had never thought of it. Now we could make love, we had the opportunity. And now we had to. Only later, very much later, did I experience our sexuality as something "transcendent". In this sense we created each other to love.'

How do you interpret celibacy and sexuality now in comparison to your own earlier feelings about it and what the church teaches about it?

Ralph: 'I've already said a lot. I now see celibacy far more as a possible threat; it can be a prison for idealists who put their own needs behind diaconal or pastoral work. That can be done, but it needn't be. I also know completely mature celibate people who are emotionally quite whole and have a splendid influence. But in that case it that has to be based on a deep and sensitive prayer life or deep friendships. I had both, but I also escaped from myself. Through my contact with Joanna, this budding and fulfilling friendship, I began to blossom. Earlier I felt above all secure in celibacy. I was unattainable, and so I was there in the midst of countless young women and girls. The vow gave me a kind of protection which others respected. I was untouchable, although of course people made attempts. But I sometimes also had difficulties with my sexuality, I remained aloof and didn't enter into any relationships.

The teaching of the church has never left me unfeeling. Certainly from the beginning of my pastoral work I've been very dynamic in doctrinal thought. People and their personal consciences have always come first for me. In this sense I've never felt guilty or a sinner, even in my sexual relationship with Joanna, although that deviated from what the church regards as moral. I knew and felt that we were very honest and respected each other. And so I felt reassured and safe.'

Ralph, would you opt for celibacy again today? 'I would no longer choose it. It has brought me much that is rich, but evidently my choice was not sufficiently anchored in a healthy emotional life. And fortunately the mid-life crisis unmasked that. I've now learned to cope with it and can develop my love life much more healthily and openly.'

Joanna, what do you think of celibacy? 'When I encountered celibacy for the first time, for me it was directly in the context of Ralph, my own friend who "didn't keep to it". Now that I've experienced his world at close hand, I've found that we aren't unique. I mean that there are not many priests without a woman friend. A relationship with a priest is still one of the last tabus in the Netherlands. Despite the fact that there is now more room for such a relationship, there's a thick mist of secrecy around it.'

Ralph, can you say what the attraction of Joanna is for you?

Ralph: 'I feel akin to her. She attracts me by her open attitude, her warmth and art of being close to people. She is honest and consistent in choices. She is ready to be matter-of-fact, to remain down-to-earth. She's loyal. She seeks a real commitment on the basis of her conviction. She can be detached, choose for herself, can love others. She gives space and makes no claims. She is amazingly loving and has a great need for passion. You can talk well with her; she's independent, doesn't hold back behind me; she's a feminist, intent on emancipation, also in liberating thought about the world; she puts her money where her heart is. She's one in a thousand. And I have the feeling that only she can make me happy, give me rest and make me develop. She gives me the home that I needed so much; she keeps me young. And I have the feeling that she takes me seriously, even needs me.'

Joanna, what is attractive to you in your relationship with Ralph?

Joanna: 'Ralph was the one who led me to experience new things. As far as the church is concerned he has opened up a new dimension for me. We draw our strength from the same source. That makes us akin at the deepest level.

I find him an effervescent man, no threshold is too high for him; he radiates an enormous amount of stimulation and enthusiasm. He's a source of inspiration for others; power flows from him and he is incredibly loyal to his own choices. I think that he has finally found himself through me. Dares to think of himself, as a result of which he can become a new person. It's tremendously attractive if you can experience that as a person. Look, he's my mate, with an enormous sense of humour!'

Do you think that it can go on, a woman living together with someone who is a priest?

Ralph: 'I think that there are priests with women friends who can do this. I know some. But I can't. I don't want a relationship which constantly makes me tense, a relationship in which my woman friend has to be tabu, hidden, known only to our most intimate friends. I want equality, openness, honesty. I don't want to go on living in the anxiety that a conflict might possibly break out with the church authorities. For the moment we can't expect any change in the law. Moreover I myself can't live with this duality: totally give myself to Joanna as a priority and at the same time continue to do pastoral work to which I was "married" for fifteen years, with its exclusive demands. I cannot and will not bear this tension. Morever, my heart needs psychological repose in order to build up a totally new way of living with a close relationship, two people thinking and living together. For that I want time and inner concentration. I've staked everything on this, because it mustn't go wrong. I've also seen too many pastors escaping into a new relationship without being well prepared for it. My departure from priestly work belongs to the phase of building up a relationship with Joanna. As a believer too I've become more of an exile, more a seeker who has less protection and cover in church and ministry. And yet I feel good, splendid in this process.'

Joanna: 'I think that it can only work if there is a future in it. If there were no prospects of a bit of freedom, for me it would mean that there was no possibility for growth. Then you can only move through a fixed framework. No, I'm grateful for that.'

How do you see the future for yourselves?

Ralph: 'We hope to grow into a deepening relationship. After a few months, when we've found a house, we shall begin to live together, as a logical next step. After around a year we hope to get married. We very much want a family. We believe that we can do this together. We certainly know that we shall constantly go on talking to each other, not least because of the difference in our ages. We both have many friends, liberating relationships and acquaintances. That can easily make our home an open one, in the sense that our relationship will be increasingly open to others. We now also want the responsibility of children. Also because I've been able to get a good job with favourable conditions for a family. We don't want to wait too long for that. I have no ambitions to return to pastoral work, not least because I think that my commitment can be fulfilled in my new functions. Joanna may also perhaps have a chance to use her qualities in the sphere of work. At all events, I want to investigate that with her. Our relationship mustn't degenerate into a house, a garden and a pet. We don't want that, and the past years haven't been like that.'

Joanna: 'Ralph has very clearly given the main outlines of our future. We've had a good run of several years. At my request Ralph is going to live alone for a while. In the end I too have spend five years in rooms. After that there will be an exciting time: getting to know each other again, living together under one roof. I'm looking forward to the first year of renewed acquaintance and friendship. I also hope that together we can create an "open house" which others can share. But we need this first time alone very much.'

How do you see the future of the church?

Ralph: 'I'm gloomy about the future of the church as an institution. In the West it will get much smaller. But in the rest of the world it will have an explosive growth and become a powerful social factor. The Catholic church in the Netherlands will begin to change considerably in structure: large-scale management and associations, smaller-scale communities. But the flame will be kept alive. And more justice will be done to ministries and tasks, despite opposition from Rome, above all those of the laity. In the next century I expect a new period in the development of religious questions here in the West. But first of all many sacred cows will have to be disposed of in the institution. Not much pressure will be needed for this. They will disappear of their own accord. The conflict with Rome will become even greater, but ecumenism at the grass roots and in actual life will grow, despite the institutions. There will be more consideration for the private life of pastors. More attention will be paid especially of the spiritual health of priests, through a better legal status. Celibacy may for the moment continue to be an obligation attached to the priesthood, but in time to come the friendly relationships of priests will be more acceptable and it will be possible to discuss them. I don't expect that in the long run the leaders of the church in the Netherlands will practise discrimination and actually expel people.'

Joanna: 'If you compare the church with a business, it has the worst personnel welfare you can imagine. I'm thinking of the position of priests, women, young people, the young unemployed. If the church really wants to stay in the picture, then the doors and frameworks must be open. Furthermore, there will be a church in many forms; sometimes something new will emerge, the torch will be handed on.'

On the basis of your own situation, have you any advice to give to a couple in a situation like yours?

Ralph: 'I don't think you can give any advice. For me the priority is that striving for a relationship of equality is very important. I could never tolerate a woman friend having constantly to stand in a subordinate role because of the priesthood. You can't allow a situation which goes against human dignity to continue. For all kind of reasons, getting out isn't a sound solution. I think that pastors with an intimate relationship must get together, talk to one another, and with a few bishops. They are primarily shepherds, listeners, bridge-builders. A climate of reflection must be created as a first step to some spiritual health for so many priests who sit silent.

From my side I no longer want to be involved in this phase of fighting and conquering. I don't want to continue a stressful fight that goes on for years. So I've chosen to leave pastoral work. But that's a choice, partly out of helplessness because I want an honest relationship with Joanna as man and wife, and partly because inwardly I've grown away from the spirituality of the ministry. I've turned into a searching believer who wants to preach and preside less, to listen and be with people more. I would advise couples in any case to talk to each other, and also to those in the same position, without a political attitude but listening to ways of making a contribution to spiritual health. And that certainly goes for priests.'

Joanna: 'I would want to advise others not to get stuck in their own stories. Look for friends, together and separately, who understand the situation, to whom you can open your hearts. See that you don't get isolated with your own problems. Show clearly what you want from your relationship, what your expectations are. In that way there's less chance that you'll have great disappointments.'

Do you see yourself as innovators, people on the way to a new form within the church, or as people who have been compelled to go down a side track?

Ralph: 'I see us as people who have opted for the side track. Tired of fighting, seeing no more sense in years of tensions and confrontations, we've opted for a new way of living, together, without constantly having to live in a kind of ambiguous role.

But we're only innovators in a very small way. Perhaps in the sense that we've dealt very carefully with our relationship, that step by step we've grown towards decisions that we can now make with heart and soul and that we've tried to do justice to humanity and equality.

I don't have the feeling that I've left office for Joanna. With her I've grown into a new content of life which suits me very well. I find it difficult that the church no longer finds any room for me in office because I have a woman friend, but I suppose that for the sake of my own spiritual rest and in order to be able to construct a good new future, I've opted for a different kind of work from the pastorate, in which otherwise I could have continued to function. In pastoral work you often take on great psychological pressure, an enormous workload in the evenings and at weekends: that isn't a helpful climate for us if we want to have a family. We shall have to do some hard thinking.

Perhaps, though, there is something renewing in this sense: that young people should get the opportunity of devoting themselves for a number of years to church work in a sort of contractual relationship, also with a clear ministry, but without a lifelong tie or an obligation to celibacy.'

Joanna: 'Yes, I see myself as an innovator. We aren't just on a side track. We're looking for a new beginning. For me, being on a side track is something that you allow to happen. We haven't done that; we've just looked for as creative a solution as possible. If Ralph sees himself on that side track, I think that he is seeing himself in his function within the institutional church. Socially speaking, we're completely involved in the church. We also find that by talking a lot about our relationship we've made other people think. So we've brought about a conscientizing. And at any rate that's innovative!'

What's different in this relationship for a woman from an 'ordinary' relationship?

Joanna: 'I can't "just" be happy. As a woman you have to be able to define your position in this relationship more than in another relationship. You have to stand up for yourself more, be more alert. All kind of processes of concealment are involved, so you have to be alert. Your relationship isn't obvious. It's often handing over responsibility to others. Nor can you just pass over the tradition and the education of a priest. In this sense as a woman you stand "empty-handed".'

Ralph: 'I think that in our case it's very different. But at the heart of the matter it's about an inner dialogue, not just in theory, a constant being in love, a game without limits. And that is just as it is in other relationships. Of course the difference in age counts, but we've found a way of bridging this. Sometimes it will still prove that I've lived a celibate life for a long time, above all in the sense that I've thought on the basis of my own agenda. But Joanna feels all this much more sharply.'

You've gone through a very intensive process in recent years. When you look back on it, are there guidelines or conclusions that you think important?

Ralph: 'I've already said a lot about the positive things between Joanna and me. Our relationship has been a catalyst, although this chemical term doesn't do justice to our emotions and the intimacy that there is between us. I've learned a lot from it, but that isn't perhaps so evident. But I would like to mention a few things:

– As a pastor, take time for friendship, for enjoying without guilt feelings.
– As a pastor, dare to be honest about your sexual feelings.
– Cultivate your prayer life and your feelings for God.
– Don't hide behind commandments and prohibitions and don't engrave your vows on stone.
– See that you can discuss intimately with colleagues or some friends.
– Don't enter into any relationship in which you can't be faithful to what you arouse in the other person.
– In the first place you're a human being, a believer, a seeker: accept that in this respect you're very vulnerable in ministry and that you can't hide behind eternal promises.'

Joanna: 'I would want to say at least this to other women in a similar situation.
– Be alert!
– Don't be afraid of standing up for yourself.
– Talk with other women.

– Don't swallow your sorrow, pain or anger, but let it out.'

Ralph, what is it like to be acting completely different from what your boss, the institutional church, expects of you?

Ralph: 'Now I feel that it's a liberation, though inwardly I still have to let a lot go, since the priesthood has also grown in me, in my blood and veins. But I feel threatened by periods of anxiety. I shall no longer be bowled over by condemnations, or get any answer to a request for a dispensation from the vow to celibacy. I know precisely how I have gone my way with Joanna, how conscientiously we have made decisions. It is not that the church as boss (what a hard word) leaves me cold, but I'm not an instrument without a will. I've stood heart and soul in office, and now I've handed back this task. I didn't expect any painful ingratitude for this, although I don't expect a distinction either. But I don't feel guilty or one who has broken trust. On the contrary. Moreover, what I want to devote myself to and what I am no longer motivated to has become clear from what has been said above. That doesn't mean that I shall lose my spirituality or inner resistance or let it be drained away. But I now want to channel it specifically into a non-church function, though with an educational dimension. Critical solidarity seems to be the pointer, and that seems more liberating than being a priest-in-office.

I shall always bear the marks of having been a priest for fifteen years. I'm not going to avoid that or suppress it; I've found very great joy and happiness in it.'

'If we keep to this aspect, we reduce the crisis of the religious life to a crisis of identity, a crisis, moreover, that would affect those attempting to define it more than those living it out. And that is in fact is what one reads and hears everywhere, from the Vatican to the smallest religious group. In my view the crisis in question is much deeper than a crisis of identity, and it primarily affects those who live the religious life. It is not a matter of knowing how to define oneself in relation to points of reference which remain completely unchanged or have been superficially renovated in the style of the day. What we have is a transformation of the landmarks themselves, a transformation so radical that they no longer serve as landmarks or mark out quite a different route – that is, when they do not seem to bar the way altogether or lead one to wander round in circles. The crisis is not over the identity of the religious life but over the representation of God, of humanity, and the relationship between them. The question of the religious life as a state can only be raised again (at this point I am not talking about what individuals or small groups can undertake according to their needs and their pleasure, though this is the most interesting and most important thing!) when we have new views of God, humanity and their relationship.'

(from Jacques Pohier, *God in Fragments*, p.30)

Slow metamorphosis

I retreated into a monastery
and lived in it many years.
I was full of the greatest ideals,
but had to let them go,
for mediaeval ways of life
which were then still fresh
can no longer be kept
in today's plastic bag.

I also looked thoroughly
for new packing materials
until I found the content rotten.
Now I no longer
have a habit
and so struggle through long empty
pages of life
to stand up weary and crippled
from tatters of beautiful church music,
and pallid mediaeval goblins.

Leo van Hamersfeld

The other side of reality

Leo van Hamersfeld was a priest. At a particular moment in his life he left the priesthood. His monastic life had set him thinking. He wrote an autobiography, about new insights which arose and old values which died. Leo is an effervescent man, an artist who has the art of living. His story gives insights into the life of a priest.

'I want to hand on to others what with difficulty I began to see as precious in my life, indeed as extremely precious. I want somehow to bear witness to it.'

Leo was ordained priest in 1950. He left the monastery 'for a woman'. At least that's what it looked like to outsiders. His departure was preceded by a process lasting years. You don't 'just' fall in love, and don't 'just' leave the monastery.

Here are some fragments of his story.

Leo was five years old when his mother died. Perhaps because he was still so small, that hardly caused any break in his life. He sees his youth as an uncomplicated child's life.

'Later I often asked myself what the role of my mother had been in my life. I didn't know her, don't know what she expected from life, how she thought about life and death, and what her marital relationship with my father was. Later I heard about the inhibited ideas about sex which he had and put into practice. Tenderness and romance were certainly not on the agenda of fanatical Roman Catholic married life. This was something that was to determine my youth and later life. My mother had died a saint. That was communicated to us in all shapes and forms. When we went to bed there was always an aunt or a maid there and a particular prayer was said that was printed on my mother's "in memoriam" card. On the card was a nice photograph, taken after she had died and lay smiling peacefully with a nun's cap on, a black habit and a great white cross on her breast.

She was buried in the habit of the "third order of St Francis". My father, who was a glazier and sculptor, put manufactured, coloured, lifesize plaster images of mother's face in the nun's cap all over the house. Father lived like a monk, meditated, and devoted particular times of the day to spiritual reading. Of course I didn't understand any of this, but shared the admiration which everyone had of him. My mother's holiness was instilled in us as a dogma. She had had intimations which came true, and that only happens with saints. The details of these were never told us, though she had spoken of her children. "Remember that you are to be brave and loving," was instilled into us, "for Mama predicted that otherwise one of you would be bad and go to hell." '

Leo was brought up with the classical sense of sin in which hell was clearly always present as a result of mortal sin.

'Yes, I was that sinner. As a joke I once made the boy who sat next to me in the first class of school feel my penis which had stuck out through a hole in my trousers. He was shocked and called me "sinner", though he had laughed at this. When I made my first communion of course I had to tell this in my first confession so as not to go to hell.

That first communion in my sixth year was indeed a hell of anxiety for me, because I then knew that I had already committed mortal sins of unchastity and because I didn't dare to tell them to the pastor to whom I had to confess and for whom I was a server at mass.

But it was the naked breasts of my mother that I had seen as a child which, despite everything, gave me the beginning of a more balanced insight into these things. I had a secret, and that couldn't be a sin. My mother was a saint and so her bare breasts couldn't be unchaste and sinful, and it must be also the same one way or another with the penises that we had.

The typical feature of these youthful experiences was that they have now given me the insight that power and power-structures in our society are inextricably connected with the sense of guilt, conflicts of consciousness and solitude which result from them.

The Roman Catholic church had me in its power, just as it also had everyone else in its power, by the sense of guilt that was instilled in us. The sense of sexual guilt is *par excellence* capable of giving every individual the idea that he or she is an exception.

Later I came to discover that those in office can also be bowed down by those same ideological means of power. The creepy thing is that the means of power seem to have become as it were a separate entity, detached from human individuals. So it is impossible to point to any individual who is responsible for the consequences.

Those who brought me up, my pastor, our maid and the church authorities, are not to be blamed for the suffering they imposed on small children. These things are much more complex. It is important to realize that it is a slow process for an individual to grow out of the sense of sin that is inculcated and impressed on you in youth.'

In the family it was decided that the three sons should become priests. There was also a plan for Leo to go to a private junior school in the south of the country.

'As was the custom then in Catholic circles, children were often predestined to a celibate life within the hierarchical structures of that institution. My youth was a final example of this. Great changes took place in my life which set me apart from others around me and their values. The very milieu from which I came became very different.

I have always been intrigued by the question precisely when my own self-conscious choice came to replace the pressure of my surroundings and I began to choose for myself.

My father's choice fell on H, and in August 1935 I was there, in that far south, deep in Brabant, caught up in a new world. A new phase in my life began.

In H there were different categories of inmates in a great complex of buildings. They lived in strict segregation from each other and hardly caught sight of each other. I was one of the so-called "pensionaries", the elite body of paying inmates, largely from Brabant and Limburg but also from other regions of the Netherlands, Belgium and the Dutch East Indies. These were all rich people's children. Somewhere else in the immense complex of buildings there should also have been the orphans, children without parents. Later, when I was at the minor seminary, it became clear to me that it was a division with children of parents who were less well off. A fellow student whom I had never seen in those college years told this to me. His father was just a policeman, and all these "orphans" were ordinary boys like us, he said. There was also the so-called "juvenate" of older boys with shaven heads. There was secrecy all around me. Later I could discover the parallels in our gatherings. Power structures seem to have an essential need to create a background of anxieties, secrecies, mysteries, conflicts of conscience, not being able to express feelings of inferiority through the incomprehensible technical language (Latin, for example) which was used by the "initiated" and the "specialists".

In the dormitory, the room in which we slept, I had my own little alcove, a small wooden bedroom with lattice work above, a kind of latticed prison cell. When we went to bed, the brother on watch came along and closed all the little rooms on the outside. Later I asked myself what would have happened had fire broken out. We were shut up in our sealed cages like rats in traps.

One evening when I put my head out above the prison, I saw another head appear. We waved at each other and began to throw bits of paper. More heads appeared, but they included that of the brother on watch, who later opened the catch of my door when I was again under the bedclothes. He came in, put his hand on my head and asked me please to be quiet and go to sleep gently, otherwise he would have to punish me, and he didn't want to do that.

He spoke in a gentle whisper and he had a nice warm hand, not wet but dry and gentle, like Papa's, and he stroked my cheeks and my neck.

During the following week he again came quietly into my room, gave me a piece of chocolate and asked how I found things in H and whether I was homesick. He said that I must be a brave boy. And just like father he made the sign of the cross on my forehead and on my bare back and breast. I thought him especially nice.'

Leo made friends, the boys were interested in his stories. They played tricks, did things that were forbidden, usually childish things. And something else happened, somethng that is less clearly forbidden, precisely because it's a mixture of warmth and something secret.

'At that time the brother on watch would come round to my room regularly in the evening, bring a sweet or some cake for me, sit on my bed and begin to stroke me all over, in a particular order: my face, my neck, my back and chest and finally between my legs. Finally the order got shorter and in the end he fumbled especially in my crutch. He did this very lovingly and gently. He kissed me. He always put his breviary behind my head on my pillow.

He whispered in a heavy Brabant accent. It was about temptations to unchastity and had to do with my penis. It had become clear to me that if this became erect it was a temptation to unchastity. But how could that be with this holy brother, for I found that his gentle fumbling in my underwear, in which he touched my penis in a very effective way, gave particular pleausre, making my member stiff and erect, and that was precisely what was wrong, that was precisely the sin of unchastity. I didn't want it, but found it great; it was wrong, but the brother himself did it... It was very strange and schizophrenic.

Fortunately I wasn't too oppressed by it and at home only said that this dear brother was friendly and very loving towards me. Father made a very nice drawing for him. I was happy to be able to give this nice picture of his patron saint to this brother, but found it strange that by day he didn't seem to acknowledge me and didn't even thank me for the nice work of art that my father had made for him. It also seemed as if he was afraid of me. I was tossed to and fro between guilt feelings about and not having been unchaste.'

After two years in H, Leo decided to go to NK. There he encountered a quite different life. Despite the great seriousness, he felt at home. Gregorian chant had a great attraction for him.

'It was solemn, splendid and impressive. The father organist accompanied in a remarkably musical way. I also wanted that life; later, it began to be my aim.

In fact I began to think of my future and ask myself whether my own will coincided with what those around me thought that

I should want. I didn't particularly feel myself "called" by the Holy Spirit or whoever.

I began to become interested in the intentions of people around me. I began to listen to my father, to what his aims were, to listen to others more critically and debate all kinds of problems with my fellow-students.

I was proud of aspiring to an authentic monastic community. Of being friendly with the superior, who had my special affection, as he was my father and mother at the same time. He always kissed me on my mouth. I didn't like these wet kisses and kept my mouth shut. He was always disconcertingly fond of me, really like the brother on watch in H, though, small as I then was, I found something strange about this brother. That certainly wasn't the case with this prior. I trusted him completely. Once in the very first year he asked me whether I knew where children came from. I knew that and could tell him in detail. And I could tell a good story, though my story was far from complete. Especially the role of the father was not yet completely clear to me. He filled in the missing details in such a natural and disarming way that none of this seemed particularly strange to me. Later I told him when I had had my first "wet dream" and had thus become a man, something that we both celebrated with a glass of sherry. I also talked to him about my sin of unchastity with a girl. He then looked very serious and concerned and wanted to know all the details. I told him that at home at my suggestion I had once watched a girl-friend from next-door making a puddle before my amazed eyes and I had looked at her in an extremely interested way. He burst out laughing, slapped me on the shoulder, and said disarmingly, "But that's not unchastity, boy! Our dear Lord made girls and boys that way." When I asked him what unchastity really was he gave me vivid examples of it: rape and incest, no more.'

When Leo was fifteen he got an injury in his eyes and had to go home to recover.

'At that time G and M took pity on me. I went around a lot with these girls. I felt strongly attracted to G. I recall how G was sitting on her bicycle and I went to sit behind her. I had my hands round her middle when I suddenly discovered that she was a woman, with a slim waist and nice round hips. All at once I fell in love with her, at least became aware for the first time that I was in love with her.

In September 1942 I went with a group of classmates to the fathers in X. I was eighteen and had idealistic ideas about "contemplation" and the monastic ife. At that time I only wanted to enter the monastic order if I didn't have to be ordained priest and, as was customary, go into parochial work. I saw this as being in principle irreconcilable with the life of a contemplative monastic order.

I had learned to take a critical look around me and noticed that there were people who went into the monastery with a terrible lack of real motivation. In fact they entered it only as an easy way of being able to lead a life as worldly clergy, free, with no ties, in a pastorate of their own, above all with food and drink and care right up to the grave.'

There were difficulties on Leo's way to becoming a good monk, like falling in love. Other girls than G aroused his love and there was also a first awareness of the reality of monastic life.

'We got up at quarter to four and were in church at four, but of all these older fathers only a few appeared; the rest stayed lazily in bed. In fact no one was interested in the night office, the prime task of a monk. There were only some whom I found to be consistent in what to my eyes was a fundamental attitude. My great annoyance at the lax attitude was really the beginning of the shift in my views about contemplation and monasticism. As far as women were concerned, I thought that one could give a kind of Platonic answer. I loved G and all these other girls, so as far as they were concerned I had to give myself a spiritual task. Loving couldn't be a sin because God himself was love: that was my simple steadfast conviction. I very deliberately set myself this task: I prayed with great ardour for my love and my girl-friends. My impulse towards renewal was inspired by this, and here I felt happy and fortunate.

In my leisure time I did some composing and sometimes even played the organ. The organist of the monastery appointed me deputy organist, along with a classmate who also played the piano. In turns we had the task of accompanying the choir.

For me these were years of exceptionally hard work, working in the garden, hoeing, shearing, feeding sheep and cows, bricklaying and building, scrubbing and polishing floors, washing clothes and doing the daily bowl of potatoes deep down in the cold, dark cellars of the monastery.'

When he was nearly twenty, Leo was 'professed', the first official acceptance into the hierarchy of the church structure. Higher studies began. The philosophy teacher laid the basis for Leo's later capacity to relativize intellectually, something of which he only became aware much later. The philosophy lessons made a great impression on him, but his uncertainty also increased: the picture that he had of himself was so unlike the one that others had of him.

'Now and then it came through to me that something was going on. I had become a "Reverend". Eyes were directed towards me outside the monastery. That had never happened before. Was I worth it, I asked myself? Because I now wore a habit, was I different from that constantly seeking boy, seeking for certainties in myself? I was very certain of all kinds of things outside myself. There was one God, Christ was his Son, the Catholic church was and had the only truth, my monastic ideal was with absolute certainty the most attractive thing I could imagine, but great uncertainties grew in me. I couldn't express them.

I thought of theology as the crown of philosophy, but it seemed nothing but disconcertingly dry and casuistic squabbles about commandments and prohibitions in human action and then *par excellence* about sexuality and marriage. From now on, when I went through the impressive, thick books of "moral theology", I couldn't avoid the impression this was a presentation of precisely what Christ had fought against so passionately with all his being, scribal learning and casuistry, and this was really casuistry carried to absurd extremes. That feeling has never left me, and moreover it became the main reason why I later turned my back on the whole structure of the Christian church.

I had fallen in love again, with the sister of an older monastic brother. She lived in the guest house with her brother, mother, older sister and a sister who was still very young. Her father had died, and they had lost their home because of the devastation of the last war. One of my own classmates was also in love with her and rivalry began between the two of us for the favours of this girl.'

Leo expressed his many loves in portraits and drawings. Love of a platonic nature. He accepted his loves and saw them as something creative and liberating.

'Then something incredible suddenly happened. On a sunny noon in the autumn of 1948 there was a sudden invasion of the monastery by pot-bellied church dignitaries. They were foreigners. Rome intervened directly. Classes were forbidden, the telephone was cut off and until further orders everyone had to stay in his room. The prior was seized in T, where he was staying with his family, and taken abroad in a car from an abbey in Belgium. Over the following days and weeks everyone in turn was put on the mat for interrogation by a church tribunal about the homosexual and paedophile tendencies of the prior. It was a disconcerting time. A completely different governing body for the monastery was set up which existed merely *pro forma*. In fact a Belgian prelate appointed by Rome was the one who held sway. The impact of this time on my life had several consequences. Again a world collapsed. For me the prior was certainly more than a superior. He had taken the place of my dead father. The loving and innocent kiss and embrace from my student days had given place to adult encounters. Complete mutual respect and appreciation had taken the place of a kind of parent-child relationship. This man had become my friend and counsellor. From a confessor he had developed into much more. He was the only person in my life who had the key to my inner being. To him I entrusted my idealism, my doubts, my life. And now he had been removed and I had to see him as a sinner...

I couldn't do this, I didn't want to. There must be something fundamentally wrong on the other side, the side of Rome...

Was that the case? Wasn't the fault with me? The last years before my priesting were a hell for me. I got hypertense and had to rest on doctor's orders.'

In 1950 Leo was ordained priest. For anyone else that moment is a milestone in life.

'I no longer recall the ordination. The most remarkable experience that I had was that my life was not "over", as evidently seemed to be the case for those around me. I heard people finally expressing the feeling "I've got there", achieved what I wanted to achieve. I noticed nothing of that.

I escaped from the consequences of my doubt in artistic activities and was given a studio in the gatehouse. I had been given a commission to make some stained glass windows for a church in Z. My brother L and I developed one of my father's processes further. Commissions followed from a missionary bishop in New Guinea to draw three sets of fourteen stations of the cross. These were forty-two great olive-green drawings. In short, there followed a time of intense activity in the artistic sphere. I earned money for the monastery. I was doing something useful for my fellow monks. I felt that my life in the monastery was meaningful.

In coming years I began increasingly to note some defects in my artistic ability. I felt attracted to graphic techniques and to the representation of figures. The female nude came up, and here I had difficulties. The male nude was no difficulty for me. I knew my own body and its anatomical expression. In my studio I had a full-length tailor's mirror and was my own model. But I had to guess at the female nude and reconstruct it by analogy with the male. I had no photographic material of women available anywhere around.

With great diffidence I showed my efforts to a fellow artist. For a moment he sat somewhat perplexed at my efforts. "Don't be offended at my sitting here so amazed, but you've never drawn a nude woman. That's quite obvious," he told me.

I was ashamed. I knew that he was right and hid my efforts deep down in my drawing chest.

Everything to do with nakedness and nude works of art, certainly relating to female nudity, seemed deliberately to have been excluded from the monastery library, made unrecognizable or rejected. It was really too crazy. On my next vacation in B I told my difficulties to my aunt and took her into my confidence. She had once had lessons from my father, could draw well, and had meanwhile brought a series of splendid daughters into the world, about whom of course I was also crazy.

That going on vacation was also something that really didn't belong in a contemplative monastic life, but was taking increasingly fixed forms in our monastery, and for a long time I myself had had no hesitations about it. On the contrary, for me it was the only possibility of getting some knowledge "in the world" which was impossible in the isolation of monastic life, or, as I later began to see, was kept from me precisely by that isolation.'

He got the chance to draw a model. Of his first female model he writes: 'She was the most beautiful thing that I had seen in my life up till then. She seemed to me an angel come down from heaven. She was so serene, so lovely, so marvellously attractive, that I was almost in paradise. However, I had no time for reflections and made the very most of the chance that had been offered me.'

That was the beginning of a new outburst of artistic activity. Leo made a name for himself outside the walls of the monastery. Not as a priest but as an artist.

'In my studio I had life-sized nudes of an attractive, long-haired, fairy-like girl and of a twenty-four-year old well-endowed adult woman. At this time I had many visits to this studio from my fellow monks, who in the first instance entered with some excuse, evidently not to look at the attractive life-sized drawings, though they seemed to do this all the more avidly when I drew their attention to them, and enthusiastically began to talk about the beauty of the nude human body, in this case the female body.

Cautiously I began to point to the obsessive state of celibate church households and the tabu that prevails around sexuality and thus around nudity. In this way barriers and prejudices were removed. Interesting conversations began to develop in my workshop and personal friendships were born.

Meanwhile L had become an adult woman and had gone into nursing. I began to fall in love with her. I visited her parents regularly; they regarded me as their stepson. At the same time I was their counsellor. Each of them took me into their confidence. I learned their marital problems, his and hers.

I regarded L as my chosen beloved, and told her and everyone else this. Pointing to her splendid photo on my desk, I even called her 'my platonic beloved'.

I wrote sonnets and other poems for her. Everyone knew of my friend L and her portrait that stood on my desk. My studio in the gatehouse came to be used for something else and I was able to set up a studio in the old part of the monastery. It was a large room which at the same time became my home. I made it as friendly as possible, but chose striking places for the most attractive life-sized nudes.

I don't know the immediate occasion, but I was asked to come to the abbey of the Trappists at T to get to know some art-loving brothers there. A lasting contact was established, in which for some years I gave a lesson to one of the fathers in drawing from models. There too the lesson turned into heated disputes with an increasing number of celibate "loners" who were in some distress.

As an opponent of the secrecy about sex which surrounded me everywhere I had become a deliberate blabber. I spoke out about my emotions and my thoughts. This was evidently much valued by individuals; brothers and laity took me into their confidence when they were alone with me. In the midst of the attractive nude women on paper, in my studio all kinds of misery in the sexual sphere was made clear to me.

I was asked at the college to give lectures in the history of art, and I again took up my old love, the study of philosophy. My artistic work faded into the background. I began to write more, got involved in an extended correspondence with a wide variety of people and was asked to write articles for various papers.

The contemplative stress on being turned inward, introversion, the withdrawal into monastic life, became increasingly alien to me. I found travelling and life with a busy agenda much more interesting and impressive.

As cantor organist of our abbey, along with some other brothers for years I was responsible for the Sunday High Mass and Vespers broadcasts from the Catholic radio station in Hilversum. I got connections with the radio world and took part in a radio programme from there. I had a full timetable and enjoyed myself, despite the increasing conflict deep in my thoughts. However, I suppressed all doubts and uncertainty.

One morning the abbot came to me while I was going down the corridor as if to make a passing remark: "Father Leo, beginning today you have the *jurisdictio ordinis*." I put my hands to my head, because that meant that a pastoral and in this case a "magistral" function was being assigned to me, without a slow and elective process of growing through increasingly senior church functions and climbing up the ladder of the church hierarchy.

I was too amazed to be proud and laughingly asked to what I owed this honour. "You'll see one of these days," he said smiling. A few days later thre was a knock on my door and one of the younger brothers came in. Suddenly I thought again of the jurisdiction I had just got for nothing and through which I was officially appointed to be a confessor to priests. I thought: "O yes, this one comes to tell me that he has left and so... and this one because I have quite open ideas about things." It was indeed he who had asked the abbot for my jurisdiction.

The jurisdiction that I had involved me directly in many "morning clients", as I called those who soon after beginning church life came to get a clean soul, freed from guilt complexes and a sense of sin because they masturbated.

Very deliberately, but O so carefully, I tried to give them another conviction about unchastity and sexuality, when they came to "confess" to me in the early hours of the morning.

I had to be extremely careful, because I was going directly against official Roman teaching, although I said nothing against so-called sacramental penace and the Roman rites relating to it.

The 1960s: visit to Rome

Leo became increasingly burdened by the conflict that was taking place in him, on the one hand by his specific position as confessor to his colleagues, and on the other by the inhibiting structures. His health often let him down.

'Ecumenism and other cries were the watchwords which kept me going. I thought that my new ideal could be thinking ecumenically and acting ecumenically.'

In Rome in the framework of the Vatican Council, during a world exhibition of Roman Catholic activities, he met attractive people, those in high office, and colleagues who came to make their confession to him. He was flattered, but the same time felt that he was living in a phantom world.

'I took in very happily the atmosphere that the activities of the

Council were emanating at this time. I went my own way, approached it, entered into it and tried everywhere literally to see the other side. The Generalate where I was then staying was on the Aventine. A whole series of university buildings and general monasteries of all kinds of orders and congregations were sited about 200 feet or so above the Tiber. It's a splendidly lofty and select part of the city.

Next to the Cistercian Generalate lies San Anselmo, the university and the Generalate of the Benedictine order. I often went there and looked around, wanting to see whether the same things happened as at M and all the other monasteries that I regularly visited. I even went voluntarily to lectures in philosophy and ancient church music.

At that time I also stayed in Frossinone, about sixty miles south of Rome, and especially in "Casa Mari", a famous and splendid mediaeval monastery of the Cistercian order and thus a bit the counterpart of the Benedictine Monte Cassino on the other side of the Apennines. I was also a guest of honour there and made grateful use of this to look behind the scenes everywhere.

By preference I looked behind the scenes at times when I knew that people had to be involved in the offices or in church life. Above all during the Sunday High Masses when there were many strangers (and thus also women) in the monastic churches, you could take it for granted that ninety per cent of all male inhabitants of the monastery would be in church. I stayed both with the Benedictines in Rome and with the Cistercians here and there in Italy on such occasions, even in the cells of the fathers, to be able to compare them with those in Holland, and again noted that all over the world there were the same celibate rubbish heaps and dunghills, but also their opposite, namely painfully reflective poetic flowers...

I saw in Rome how a young priest monk shyly dodged into one of the college halls with a twelve-year-old boy when I went in almost noiselessly, and how in Frossinone another young monk disappeared just as skilfully behind a closed door with a small mass server into the luxurious garden on the hillside.

My ideas about Roman Catholic celibate life were even further confirmed by all this.

It was in this "Roman time" that the slow changes in my own

convictions which had already been growing for years suddenly accelerated.

The more time went on, the more I was put off by Roman life and then increasingly became detached from it. The whole Roman renewal which seemed to be going on during Vatican II made little impression on me. It was as if this great awakening passed me by.

I felt pity for all those around me. I knew that they took the life in which they shared extremely seriously, whereas within their rooms they lived quite a different life: a life full of anxieties and guilt complexes. I witnessed that every morning through those who confessed to me.

I didn't take that church life seriously in any respect. I simply couldn't continue with it. The only thing that I took seriously was my sketchbook, my study of philosophy and the conversations every morning and even every evening with all kinds of people. This was the time when I first really began to get anxious about my future. How was I to go on if I really had to acknowledge that I no longer believed in Roman Catholicism, and abhorred its penitential practices?

What conclusion was I to draw? Did I have to resign my office and get out of the monastery? What did I have to start on in a world which was alien to me?

I couldn't leave these poor devils morning and evening. Apart from my honesty in personal conversation I had nothing to give; I was nothing and had nothing to show. The external church glamour and involvement in it began to offend me. I saw it as a house of cards ready to collapse. What was I, and what would I get involved in if I turned my back and stepped out of it? I didn't even have anything personal to show "in the world". Was that the case?'

Leo's health got worse. He returned to the Netherlands for treatment. He got medicines – far too many, it was to prove later.

'Deep within me, however, there was yet another conflict, a life-sized conflict. I know that all too well. There was hardly anyone to whom I dared express it and I thought even then that some of my package of woes was due to this "psychological" situation of conflict. Did I have to spend the rest of my life in a sphere in which I no longer believed?

All around me the situations of conflict lay specifically at the sexual level. However, my conflict was certainly not in this area but was much deeper. For dozens of years I had ceased to have any difficulty with my celibate life-style. That was certainly not my problem.

But how could I continue this life if I no longer believed in the reason for it? "Roman Catholicism" no longer existed for me, just as Protestantism, Islam, Buddhism, Hinduism, Brahmanism and all these thousands of other -isms were no more and no less for me than very relative convictions laden with fanaticism. I no longer believed that any -ism had the right to exist or that it was dogmatically right. I increasingly thought the fanaticism with which people forced their convictions on each other to be an archaic occupation, bearing witness to a very limited self-awareness.

I became increasingly convinced that no one is in a position to pass an objective judgment. All judgments are subjective judgments. Objectivity seems to me purely an abstraction, like philosophical axioms.

My belief that the church's dogma was right had been attacked and was finished. There was a question mark against everything.

However, my good faith in medical knowledge, which was just as dogmatic, was completely intact, and this medical science which really surrounded itself, as the churches did, with the aura of exclusiveness and skill, proscribed me medicines, better and better, more and more, all different, ever more modern...

Meanwhile, at the college I undertook all kinds of ecumenical activities, also out of a collective need which had arisen to look for solutions for individual problems which were steadily growing greater.

There was propaganda for ecumenical services and taking part in them. I dragged many of my acquaintances and also members of my family to them. My nieces from B and their friends and acuqaintances were also involved. Congresses and ecumenical services were organized. I made sure that in passing my dearest women friends were also regularly around me.

It even happened once that I took these girls into the monastery and they went along to my studio and my room through the part of the monastery to which "laity", including people of the opposite sex, could have access. They included my nieces and also Annie, the girl from T.

I met Annie on one of the days when she was staying in the monastery with hair awry and crying loudly. I was shocked, took her to my room and began long conversations with her. She was keeping something secret from me and I couldn't really discover what it really was. She was fond of me and I of her. She wrote fond letters, telephoned increasingly often and for a longer time, but kept her secret.

One of my celibate friends began a kind of competition with me to see which of the two of us had the most women friends. I wasn't particularly happy about this, above all because he told me one "adventure" after another, down to the most intimate sexual details. It was 1968 and there was again some ecumenical meeting in our monastery, at which Annie was also present. Afterwards I realized that I was on the point of falling in love with her. That evening I again tried to talk about her sorrow and to discover precisely what the matter was. We had walked slowly through the gardens and had gone into the church. At a particular moment we were sitting side by side at the end of the church. I had my arm around her and was drawing her towards me. We were really gently caressing, something I didn't dare think more about, and which I found embarrassing, when suddenly it became as clear as day to me that she was one of the many "victims" of the advances of my pastoral friend. When I asked her whether this was true she burst into tears and nodded in confirmation. She seemed to have been head over heels in love with him and had had severe pangs of conscience for years which she didn't dare to express to anyone.

I was suddenly a witness to the searing sorrow which I really knew was all around me: women who have indirectly become victims of priests and of men living celibate lives for religious ideas. I very deliberately took hold of her, drew her towards me caressing and kissing her, and said, "Now it's all over. I'm going to care for you."

Suddenly I had made up my mind. I would leave the monastery

and look after Annie. She held me fast and like two lovers we sat there in the back of the church caressing.

Something had happened in a moment which I was as it were well prepared for outside myself and which in a twinkling solved my whole problem deep in my heart.

A purpose in life had been instilled in me. Away from the grasp of Rome. Leaving my monastery. Loving Annie, caring for her and finally giving her a safe home. I wanted to take this dear person whom I so admired at last out of her eternal misery.

I suddenly saw bringing a person finally out of loneliness and confirming them in love as an ideal to be realized.

That same evening I began to sort out all kinds of things prior to being able finally to leave the monastery. I didn't sleep that night and cycled aimlessly round the neighbourhood. The next morning I went to tell the abbot about my sudden decision and to make an official announcement in the monastery. On one of the next few days I called my pastoral friend and was extremely fierce to him. I was furious, and tried to make it clear to him through this affair what catastrophic things he was engaged in, because women love differently from men. This was a typical example of a kind of adoration which women could cherish for an idol and could keep alive for years. We men are always capable of being much more rationally in love than women with their characteristic emotional feminine way of loving. I argued that we were not to abuse this. What he was in fact doing was to abuse women seriously... Our friendship cooled, although we didn't completely avoid each other.

Again my life was completely changed in a few moments. Annie fell in love with me directly, because she had really loved me for six years, as her loyal adviser and faithful guardian. She began to hate my friend, her ex-friend, fiercely.

It was clear to me after that deliberate conversation with her in the church that from then on I wanted to seek her, love her and cherish her exclusively. And this was what I began to do over the course of years. I wrote a L long letter in which I set down the whole truth. I told her of my decision and why. It was a final parting from her. I said goodbye to all her family and removed her portrait from my desk.

I did the same with all the other women with whom I had had

contact. I wanted to begin a new life with a completely clean sheet and devote myself exclusively to Annie. Monogamously.

I removed my monastic name which was on a wooden board in the entrance to the monastery, as a symbol of the definitive step I had taken. From now on there was no longer any "Father Leo" in this monastery.'

Leo relates how the sudden decision to turn his back on monastic life was the hardest and most far-reaching decision in his life. For him the future was full of uncertainties. Many of his colleagues who had taken up a career in education had been able to accumulate some social security. He hadn't. Moreover his state of health was still bad. But he made a change in his life.

'It was not only another change but also another meaning. I began to think differently about church and society; about God, religion and theology. I had other ideas about authority and authoritarian relationships within society. I had fought free inwardly of a sense of sin and guilt feelings. Connected with all this, but above all through my many and intense contacts with women and my love of them, and also through my artistic activities, like giving lessons in model drawing, my many contacts with naked people, girls, boys, women and men, my views about sex, nakedness, marriage, love, falling in love, tenderness and so on had become very different from those which were still common around me. Certainly these views were different from those of the official Roman church.

I had been able to restore happiness to many people in marital relationships which had gone wrong. Above all, though, I had been able to help many people by bringing them the insight that a mediaeval institution like the Roman Catholic church, ruled by male celibates, and its Reformation offshoots, used guilt feelings and a sense of sin as a means of power *par excellence*. Threats of hell and damnation, above all centred on sexuality, which is so fundamentally mysterious for everyone, are, seen in historical perspective, the most effective means of power that people have ever found. Guilt feelings, isolation and power belong together.

The whole of our Western society has been affected by this. The reforms of Luther, Calvin and other great and courageous people were really fumbling down the same narrow street as far as these fundamental matters were concerned. In fact nowhere was anything fundamental or essential reformed; on the contrary, new distorted paradigms or ideas of life were brought into being which began to nestle alongside the existing ones. Power structures remained masculine and immature where emotional expressions were concerned.

The Calvinistic views of life, the Calvinistic image of human beings as being by definition sinful, of man inclined to sin and predestined, and of a God who judges and above all condemns, are exclusive proof of this.

It had become my firm conviction that a primarily male immaturity where emotional expressions were concerned, and all kinds of obsessive collective basic ideas about human beings themselves, were also the consequence of them within Catholicism.

I saw male supremacy and the means of power used by patriarchal institutionalism as being by definition hostile to women.

I began to see the Roman and Reformation theologies as a development from a predominantly male Greek thought through a celibate mediaeval male thought to male projections of a male God. To a high degree hostile to women.'

Leo married Annie. They loved each other deeply for twenty-two years. In 1984 Annie died of a brain tumour. Another turning point in his life, now not one that he had chosen. And again he succeeded in living meaningfully. Art remains the main thing in his life. And he writes. Writes about the things that preoccupy him. He wants to hand on his discoveries.

It seems to the world as though Annie was the occasion for Leo's departure from the church. In Annie he found a motive for changing his life, in her he discovered a new meaning. But the process of leaving had already begun years earlier. It was a constantly increasing conflict with a church system with which he could live less and less. His wrestling brought new insights.

Priests and their relationships with women

Louis Sommeling

Louis Sommeling is an ex-Jesuit. He is a psychologist and psycho-therapist attached to the Rijksuniversiteit in Groningen and a sexologist at the Rutgers Foundation there.

Introduction

After the many women who have expressed their predominantly negative experiences in their relationship with priests in this book, I want to make a contribution as 'someone who has experienced it from the other side'.

I want to say something of my experiences in this area and then give a theoretical account on a professional basis.

I'm doing this because I think that too little has been written on this subject, though it seems to me very important for all those thousands of religious and priests who are seeking their way in a changing world, whether they are still in, half out or completely out.

Even when you've closed the priory gate or the church door behind you or have left it open a chink, influences remain engraved on your soul which have a psychological effect. Self-knowledge and self-understanding are needed here. Guidance is almost completely lacking.

First I shall say something about myself, then I shall describe well-known problems in the relationship between a priest (or an ex-priest) and his partner, and then I shall sketch a theoretical explanatory model by which much can be make clear; finally I shall say something about professional help.

Personal facts

After I entered the Jesuits in 1955, regarding celibacy as a sacrifice, albeit a necessary one, it remained a lonely struggle to understand the phenomenon of women. It was only possible to talk about it when after some years I met a particularly warm woman, so that I began to experience the strange split of madonna and whore in one warm person of flesh and blood. A world opened, but no pen can describe how I finally came home, to myself as well. A warm friendship developed which gave me the courage to have myself ordained priest. But precisely as a result of this combination we failed each other, and growing expectations could never have been realized. With terrible pain in my heart I broke off the relationship. Along with friends, at the end of the 1960s I began to fight for 'married priesthood'. When it became clear that the church would never within the foreseeable future become a contemporary institution in which I and the people for whom I worked could find a stimulating message, I resolved to turn my precious energy elsewhere. I began to study psychology, married, and started a family. The aftermath of the priesthood could still be felt in my relationship for a long time. In the course of time I've begun to have a better understanding of the consequences and influences of this on my own psyche and on my relationship. This happened first of all through life with my wife and also through my study of psychology and practice as a psychotherapist. The move from the one world-picture to a completely different time and completely different life-style is so immense that much more study needs to be made of its psychological consequences, both for the priest (or ex-priest) and for those with whom he wants to enter into a relationship.

Problems of relationship

What difficulties can generally arise between a priest (or ex-priest) and his partner? Why does a man become a priest, and what consequences does this have for his sexuality and his view of women?

A man who wants to become a priest feels himself exceptional; he is a special kind of man (in theological language, he is called, he has a message for the world). He is then often accustomed to being treated and understood in a special way. This is not his own fault, because people need to see him in this way. He is often the centre of this special treatment, and sometimes he has difficulty in realizing how other people feel. But most of the time he feels that he has good intentions. This happens because he cannot bear to feel aware of normal selfish feelings and anger in this image of himself. This repression leads to his having to tell himself a nice story when he asks anything for himself. For example, 'That you are now giving me this love also helps me to understand women better; it gives me a home so that I can be a more complete person', and so on. Yet another picture which occurs often: 'I feel a universal love for all people, so I can, indeed must, love several women at once.'

He can't bear saying that he feels the urge and can also get a kick out of manipulating women and tying them to him, although this mustn't be excluded in many cases. (Why should anything human be alien to him?) Or to put it a different way: in that case he has no responsibility for his actions in welcoming women and letting them speak to him. It may be clear that in this way he can do damage to women with whom he enters into a relationship; certainly if he doesn't learn to recognize and discuss these patterns in himself. Unless he does this, he is a danger to women, all the more because it is not always chance that a woman falls in love with a priest. Sometimes women are very much struck by these sensitive, sometimes charming and apparently respectable, idealistic men. The 'togetherness' and 'authenticity' that they have missed in former relations with men (including their fathers) seem to be being fulfilled. Unconsciously, sometimes there is also the demand for the sexlessness of this new father: in any case it is a breath of fresh air to meet a man with whom you can also talk. It should be clear that here confrontations with illusory expectations must follow.

The drama of the gifted child: an explanatory model

In this section an attempt will be made to understand the ex-priest, and a model will be offered which can give some insight into the problems of relationship mentioned above.

Is it so splendid to feel yourself special as a priest, to have difficulty with the senses, always to have to smile and understand, always to see everyone's point of view, to have no recourse to your own aggression and force and always to be caught up in the half-hearted church language of 'on the one hand and on the other hand'?

Is it so great always to think that happiness is over there, behind the hill, with God or – to put it in secular terms – in someone else, and really above all in the lost paradise that you think can be found in a woman?

Always elsewhere and never in yourself. You are really an empty container, and can always console yourself with the idea that fulfilment is still to come ('Salvation is coming'). And you can deny your own emptiness with the consoling idea that you are meaningfully occupied in rescuing and saving someone else. You can give your emotions to a relationship of helping someone else. But what about your own feelings? You don't know them well, and if you did, you would feel guilty. Guilt, guilt, guilt, and who understands you? Sometimes you even begin to hate the people you're there for (you begin to impose moral demands on them, you apply perfectionist criteria, the world is bad and treats you badly).

The psychoanalyst Margaret Mahler (1975) investigated the earliest origin of the development of the feeling of self in children. She describes the subtle process by which the young child breaks the bonds with its mother and learns to make its own individual steps in the world.

Priests – like many other people – are often made particularly 'special' by their parents, sometimes with good intentions. Then we have what Alice Miller calls the 'drama of the gifted child'. Children who are made 'special' often have parents who need the child to give themselves meaning. Here the parents are often confused by the church's preaching, which not only found a 'vocation' something quite special but also made people afraid of individual thought and action, of their own power and childhood eroticism. The mother cannot bear her son to take his own independent steps into the world, away from her; it is nice if he also learns to care for her and to pay attention to her. The father is absent or approves of this mother-child relationship, from a position which is insufficiently critical and independent.

The boy does not dare to embark on the drama of separation. He gets the 'unspoken' promise from his mother, the first woman in his life: if you rely on me, and try to be special for me, then you will get my warmth, security and a home for ever. (That is why in church language the words 'together' and 'eternal' occur so often and never the words 'apart' and 'mortal'.) The child has now become the helper (the saviour of its world) and is caught up in a diabolical dilemma: if it takes its own steps and feels its own feelings (rebellion, showing its own aggression, sensuality and power) then it thinks in its infantile anxiety that it will be thrown out of its parental nest and vanish away to nothing in the dark: we can rightly call this the fear of death.

The little helper has to choose the safe way: it must note every smile of its mother, every tear and sigh, and respond with its support. It continues to be reserved for her and has to stay away from all other women.

Put at its gentlest, it is clear that the child gets ambivalent and confusing feelings for this first woman. On the one hand it longs for her promises and her paradise; on the other it has to give, becomes helpless and gets nothing really back and unconsciously gets angry. Doesn't the misogyny of the church and of human beings generally have its origin here? Now the world is stood on its head: the child has the world round its neck (hangs on the cross) instead of being borne up by this world and supported by friends and playfully lured out. To console itself for its terror and its empty feeling of self the child creates the illusion that it can comfort its mother, that it can help another person get rid of his or her sorrow: the great comforter and almighty saviour is born. The child itself is empty, but there is a promised paradise. The salvation is not in it; the power does not come from the child itself, but salvation always comes from elsewhere – from God or, in secular terms, from woman.

No wonder that many women react to such an appeal: that they have been called to be a fulfilment. That alone gives meaning to your life. Most women have also learned that. This has been clearly described by Susie Orbach (1982): women are inclined to ask for nothing for themselves, since when they tried that earlier, in their first years, they were put off, and as a result of this trauma they may well avoid risking such total negation again. They react to the appeal of the priest, they perhaps feel his deep need, all the more so since he also seems to be such an attractive, idealistic person who can also help them. And at first sight it seems as if he values women highly and supports them.

Now all the ingredients are present for a failure. Of course things can also go well or, better, good can come of it. Priests and women must learn to recognize these psychological mechanisms by confronting each other firmly and possibly by seeking professional help.

The threshold for professional help

Psychotherapy and religion sometimes seem like two enemies because – when it comes to the point – they think in terms of two different world views. Confusion, pain, failure are often interpreted in terms of a religious world as providing meaning or as part of life or as a deserving sacrifice, or as something that God asks of you. Psychotherapy does not believe that this world can be without pain, but it does believe that people can become clear about what they are doing to themselves or others, unconsciously and unnecessarily, and that they themselves can choose their own behaviour so that they can learn to be responsible for it.

The threshold to professional help is often high for people with a religious upbringing. A report by the Dutch psychologist Jos Frenken, published in 1979, shows that there are many sexual and religious problems among religious people for which no treatment is sought. I have described elsewhere how the gulf between these two worlds can be bridged, and I have also discussed a number of cases. Sometimes a psychotherapist is needed who has respect for a religious background. Perhaps a pastoral counsellor can also fulfil a mediating function by counselling and training.

Conclusion

In this article I have written about problems which often occur between priests in office who have a relationship with a woman (which is forbidden by the institute). Often this finally provokes human dramas. It damages the quality of life. It seems as if the choice has not been made properly.

When people learn to understand the background to this and thus to themselves, these problems can find a solution in human terms so that it becomes possible to have a life worth living.

The church provides too little professional help for priests and religious, for those who have left the church. The consequence of such a decisive step maintain their influence for a long time, long after people have closed the church door behind them.

Bibliography

Margaret Mahler, *The Psychological Birth of the Human Infant. Symbioses and Individuation*, Basic Books, New York 1975

Alice Miller, *The Drama of the Gifted Child and the Search for the True Self*, Faber 1983

Susie Orbach and Luise Eichenbaum, *What Do Women Want?*, Fontana Books 1984

The questionnaire

'*The oppressed suffer from a duality which is deeply rooted in their unconscious. They discover that they cannot live without freedom. And yet, however much they long for an authentic existence, they are afraid of it. At the same time they are both themselves and the oppressor that they have internalized.*'

(Paulo Freire)

Present-day morality has been preceded by centuries of a lack of appreciation for women, sometimes hidden, sometimes open. The priest-partners of the women in this book have emerged from this tradition. Some of them have grown out of it, have become aware of the patriarchal norm, and have learned to judge afresh and to see women with other eyes. Through their contacts with women others have begun to doubt the morality; their women lived in another reality and they experienced love and eroticism as an original experience.

There are priests who only after their forty-fifth birthday discover that love and sexuality have a place in their life. They make an attempt to catch up and have a late puberty, which sometimes develops into bisexuality or homosexuality. There are also priests who succeed in building an enriching, worthwhile relationship with their partners, in which both are very happy. Some have now been married for years.

The women in this book will have met men who were at varying stages of growing sexual awareness. Above all those who belonged to a monastic order first dropped an old conviction, namely that celibate monastic life is the highest, best possible form of life here on earth. In the course of history this thought was often expressed loud and clear, so that everyone was steeped in it, in the monasteries but also outside, in the world of the laity. Celibacy is part of the priestly life: the avoidance of sexuality, and that meant the avoidance of women.

'When the devil has blown the remembrance of a woman into our heart by means of his subtle deceit, to begin with our mother, our sisters and other relations, or even thoughts of some pious women, then we must drive such pictures as quickly as possible from our heart, for fear that if we dwell too long on them, the deceiver will take the opportunity of making us go on imperceptibly to think of other women.'

That is what Cassian (360-435) taught his monks.

By living a good life, i.e. a life according to the rules of the order, and thus a celibate life, one became a little better than the rest of humankind, almost a firstfruit of the hereafter. Priests became special, and ordinary people were taught to confirm this special status. Forms of address like 'Reverend' are still the remnants of this. The woman and the priest who enter into a relationship with each other bear the burden of this history, even before they are in a position to make their own history. Historical ballast, judgments and prejudices, a strictly normative education and a society which prefers not to see tabus uncovered; this is what many bring along as they take the first step together.

As one of the women says, 'You think that you're the only one, that you've been naughty because you have to keep your secret... it may never be told. It has repercussions for your partner if they (family, friends, acquaintances, parishioners, superior and bishop) get to know of it...'

People have their own opinions: the woman between madonna and whore. The woman as temptress, witch or saint. Has she 'bewitched' the priest with her charms? At the seminary a priest student is counselled at least to put a piece of furniture between himself and a woman in a pastoral converation.

It was better never to be alone with one woman. Women tempt with their bodies. Women are honoured in the Catholic church if they are virgin and so can become holy. For women of flesh and blood there is always the possibility of arranging the flowers or making the church beautiful, but the altar remains forbidden ground.

Some years ago Cardinal Simonis gave the following criticism of feminist theology: 'in the human order the priority [pre-eminence] belongs to the male.' So women are secondary, have a second place. A priest stands above a so-called lay person. According to this way of thinking a woman is a second-class lay person. Despite the attractive gloss that the woman has a 'special place', she does not succeed in getting real equality and justification, which follows from this logically.

'You are the gateway to the devil', wrote Tertullian. And Augustine thought that women probably had no souls. But all that is a long time ago. Surely we now live in another time?

'You are whores, shrews who damage the church. When these hags came to the altar, everything went wrong.' That can be read in one of the least positive letters. From another letter.

'As a man, years ago I asked myself how a woman can still be the member of an institute which down the centuries has done nothing but malign and damage women deeply. Apparently the age-old indoctrination that she is impure and imperfect has had the "desired" effect, and made her believe and acquiesce remain in her imperfection.'

Those are also questions that people are now asking.

Despite the obligatory celibacy there are nevertheless priests who enter into a relationship with a woman, a relationship which is more or less secret. Why, despite all the prejudices, judgments and condemnations? There is no answer to that question in this book. Perhaps parts of possible answers can be found somewhere, between the lines. Perhaps answers can also be found in the stories of the people in this book. These answers are in a way important, because they are the structure of the unexpressed and often unconscious expectations in which women become involved when they enter into a relationship with a priest.

'The extreme dichotomy between quasi-prophetic symbolic exaltation and social degradation of women by the Roman

Catholic church can of course be analysed in terms of compen-
sation mechanisms – compensation for the women being held
down and compensation for a celibate all-male clergy seeking
"the spiritual essence" of their rediscovered other halves.
However, I think the most important aspect of the phenomenon
has to do with the harnessing of women's power of women by
this quintessentially hierarchical and sexist institution. Es-
pecially in its periods of greatest desperation it has tried to
capture female presence and power in a symbol, using this to
captivate the psyches of women and men, mesmerizing them,
binding them in unquestioning loyalty to itself' (from Mary
Daly, Beyond God the Father *[1973],* The Women's Press
1986, pp.89f.).

The responses to the questionnaire

The women

Women who have or have had a relationship with a priest and
who took part in the questionnaire usually had a job in the so-
called soft sector. To the question 'What is your job?' the answer
was often 'I'm a district nurse' or 'social worker' or 'lecturer at a
college for social studies'. Sometimes the woman was a one-
parent mother or divorced, with children to look after. Some
women were studying theology or active in parochial work.

Of the twenty-three women who filled in the questionnaire, ten
had broken off their relationship; one woman wanted to end hers.
The average duration of the relationships is ten years. The average
age is forty-three, ranging from twenty-two to seventy-two.

What is striking is that a relationship can last quite a long time
but then come to an end. It is quite possible for the partners to
begin hopefully, thinking that they can overcome the difficulties
or cope with the problems to some degree. Finally, after many
years, 'doing your best' doesn't work. Many marriages also
end up in divorce, but the relationships described here aren't
comparable. A marriage is open and is under social control, is
embedded in the framework of family and friendship.

The majority of the women began their relationship after 1980.

They indicated that the greater openness in society and indeed in the church had little influence on the development of the relationship. Other factors were mentioned:
– working together
– new forms of religious life
– loneliness
– the view that celibacy is unhealthy.

'We sang together in the same choir. After the practices there was usually social chat.'
'I studied theology, also with pastoral work in view.'
'I applied for a job. I got it. One of my colleagues was K. So we got to know each other through our work.'

The partners of the women have an average age of fifty-five and about half belong to a religious order.

The relationship

A relationship which has to remain secret because officially it may not exist is characterized by strict divisions between what is possible and what is not. Many things that are normal in a relationship cannot be part of a relationship with a priest. This is expressed in the answers. Here are some examples:
– the secrecy business, never being accepted as a complete partner
– never being able to be together on Sundays and festivals
– the ministry comes first, you always have to share your partner
– you can't have children; the consequence of that is having to leave the priesthood
– the training/education of a priest, a celibate, sometimes makes it difficult to have a relationship with him.

Sometimes relationships are known to no one, often to a small circle of intimate friends:

'His family was never to know of my existence and everything had to be kept quiet even to his wider acquaintances.'
'For around sixteen years to be in the background, in the umpteenth place in his life, gave me very confusing feelings.'
'As for secrecy, the circle of those "in the know" constantly

increased in the last years. The order also knew about it, and asked whether he wanted to resign his office, but he didn't. Nothing happened after that.'

'Our families and real friends knew about our relationship and thought it quite natural.'

There are also women who write about their relationship, for example to the bishop.

'A few years ago I wrote to the Catholic radio station, but from their reply I got the impression that they daren't deal with this matter openly. I also wrote to the bishop. He denied that such relationships existed. I told him that I myself also had a relationship. He replied that I was living in mortal sin, but didn't concede that there were priests who have a relationship.'

There are also women who have met the bishop together with their priest friend to sound out the situation.

'I had the feeling of visiting my man's new employer. Whether we went to bed together was never discussed.'

However, many relationships are kept secret with extreme care.

'If people knew that we had a relationship, the majority wouldn't approve. They would drop us like a hot potato. We have an extra problem: he is fifty-six and I'm thirty-two. People would say that I had led him astray.'

'People often see what they want to see. They prefer not to talk about it, as though there is a collective agreement to keep quiet.'

'Whether it's in the Netherlands or in Africa, women friends are never talked about. I myself know a large number of women friends of priests, but they don't know that I'm one. They don't even know about each other.'

'You can only be a dissident in Russia. If there is one group of people on whom there is a tabu, they are those who love a priest in some way.'

'I don't always know what people think about it because you daren't discuss it. You want to let sleeping dogs lie.'

164

There are women who have a child. Often a consequence of the secrecy of the relationship is that the child doesn't know his or her father, or doesn't know that this 'uncle' is his or her father.

'When our daughter was still small, I married my present husband.'

'The problem of the children who have a priest as father isn't new,' wrote a woman who had experienced this at close quarters. 'What still makes the most impression is the constant reaction of the church authorities: the impossibility of any discussion because they deny the facts, ultimately keeping the power system going at human expense. In my experience there are three phases.

I must now think back to the 1950s, when I was working in a home for unmarried mothers. I did the administration as an assistant to the social worker. One of my jobs was to put all the facts on file. Even at that time, when no one dared to think about it, let alone talk about it, girls were being admitted who had been made pregnant by a priest. At this time the tendency was also to make unmarried mothers give up the child they expected. These women were put under pressure and received no guidance. I often involuntarily think back to this, all the more since ten years later I saw some of these women back as patients in the psychiatric institution where I was working as a counsellor. Victims of compulsion, power and hopelessness.

The facts about the relationship with a priest disappear into the famous melting pot. That usually happened by keeping it a professional secret; people used to refer to the duty to keep silent.

Moreover no proof or possible evidence can be found, since the dossier reports "father unknown". I must point out here that this happened in connection not only with priests but also with a number of well-known people.

However, it mustn't be thought that the church authorities were completely ignorant of such cases. People's lips were sealed with professional secrecy. Socially the problem had been "solved". But it was a bogus solution; the problem continued to exist.

When church people became more autonomous, we got to phase two.

There was a crisis of authority, and in the 1960s the great exodus of priests took place. Thousands left the priesthood, for different reasons. The official list of questions for dispensation for a married person was – and is – disconcertingly discriminatory, not just for the priest but also for his intended wife.

Together you went through the official mills of "the institution", which worked in a humiliating and tendentious way for both parties. We had dared to break the great tabu and along with many other people went through hell. The attitude of the church was and still is always negative. There is no place for a woman in this man's world, clearly not for the priest who marries.

That's how the problem was solved: no discussion, but getting out and keeping quiet.

When we reach the third phase, it seems that the relationships are still going on and can no longer be ignored.

To exclude a group of people doesn't mean that the problem is solved. The well-known trick of dodging the issue still works. But it's no longer possible to keep people quiet.

What I find sad is that so many women are left in the lurch by their partners and have to struggle against a bulwark of power on their own. I'm reminded of a remark by one of the Dutch bishops to a pastor friend or ours: "Here there is only one person who thinks, and that's me."

If you have to work under such a dictatorship, you have to have found great inner freedom if you aren't to become a victim of the system.

I feel a need to stand up for the women and men who risk going under in a system which shows no respect for truth and justice. It is also worthwhile helping them. I'm curious about what the next phase will look like.'

There follows a fragment from the anonymous letter of a woman who had a child.

'Fourteen years ago I worked as a volunteer in Tanzania. I came into contact with a Roman Catholic priest. First it was just friendship, but later it became love. We had a secret relationship for a number of years. I became pregnant. My world collapsed. We dicussed it. My partner wanted me to have an abortion. In his situation there was no room for a child. I didn't know what to do. Then we decided that I should go back to the Netherlands for an abortion. When it was all over I would come back and carry on with my work as usual. But things turned out differently. Once back in the Netherlands I thought of the growing child in my body. Must I, might I, have it "taken away"? I couldn't. I let the pregnancy go through and I had a son – or rather, we had a son. It was also his child. But he was far away and thought that an abortion would solve the problem. If I went back we could continue our relationship, but with better precautions against pregnancy. We had never talked about that. But I stayed in the Netherlands and looked after my son.

When he was three I married a man I had known before I went abroad. I've still kept in touch with the father of my son over the years. It was a great shock to him to hear that he had a son. Not long ago he saw him for the first time. He never talked about it to anyone. Couldn't: priests can't have children, may not have a relationship with a woman. He is still working in Tanzania as a good, exemplary priest. No one knows his secret. No one knows with what interest he reads the letters from me in which I tell him about our child.'

Such things are an enormous burden to bear. Obviously it's easier to preach from the pulpit about love than to put love into practice in the midst of a family. It's always sad if a child isn't wanted. The experience must be even more painful for a woman if the father is in the service of an organization which condemns abortion and preaches love between human beings as an ultimate good:

'When I became pregnant he insisted on an abortion, but I wanted to keep the child.'
'Now I'm alone. I often think that I could have had a child. A child whose father was a priest. But we didn't have the courage. I allowed an abortion.'

If you have a more or less secret relationship with a priest, the consequence is usually that you must give up any wish to have a child.

'Now things are fine between us. I've also reconciled myself to the fact that in this situation we shall never be able to have children.'

Living together

Maintaining a relationship is easier if you live together. From the replies to the questionnaire it emerged that this was the case in ten situations.

Living together, taking each day together come what may, can lead to a great intimacy: people learn to get to know each other better, are more familiar with each other's positive and negative sides.

If people live together there is a greater chance that a dispute will arise over defining one's own identity. However, this dispute can also limit inner growth.

Because it's impossible for the relationship to be open, a number of things are ruled out. First comes living together. There are indeed women who live openly with a priest and refuse to keep their relationship secret. Others live together, but leave ambivalent what sort of a relationship theirs is. That can be the case if someone rents rooms in a pastor's house, but it can also apply to the housekeeper.

'Of course we can't go round arm in arm.'
'When we went on vacation we were careful to take two single rooms in the hotel. You never know who you might meet.'
'We had a splendid vacation. Just the two of us together in H. No one knew us there, it was far enough away. When we got back to the station in our town it was all over. He saw the doors of the parish church and he was a priest again. Left me there with the cases.'

So it's a relationship with many limitations. A whole series of things are impossible. It's a matter of constantly new and careful searching for what is possible without taking too great risks, which can lead to the dismissal of the priest, to gossip, or to information being sent by anonymous letter to the bishop.

The negative aspect of a relationship which is more or less secret is not only the fact that the secret is hard to bear but also that there is no healthy social control. No one knows of your relationship, so no one can comment on it in ordinary life, or about the way you treat your partner or he treats you. You keep your secret and no one ever tells you that his way of treating you is strange, that it's remarkable that you do your best with all the things you don't like, in order to cover him with a mantle of love.

'There's never anyone to show you your blind spots.'
'There's never anyone to tell you what's wrong with your attitude. There's never anyone to open your eyes to the fact that his attitude is wrong, to say that you may make more demands of your partner. And the pain of being left in the lurch the moment you make demands is much more difficult to bear than when it can all be discussed more openly.'
'He was a well-known personality. Our relationship was very secret. We only saw each other at weekends. I had to read of his death in the newspaper.'

I had already asked myself whether the women were aware of these limitations, which do not occur in an ordinary relationship, when they entered into a relationship with a priest. When the relationship arose on the initiative of the priest (four times), were these limitations then expressed by him?

It could be that people began aware of these limitations to the relationship, but then found them difficult to take in practice.

The ten women with a relationship which had been broken off had maintained this relationship for around nine years.

Were agreements made in the relationship? I put this question, and got an affirmative answer fourteen times. Most of the agreement was about what was not possible in the relationship:
– not marrying, not going together to family or friends, not sleeping together, not going on vacation together, no sexual intercourse.

That fourteen women indicate that definite agreements were made may indicate that their partner was aware that his priesthood put certain limitations on the relationship. Given the official impossibility of the relationship this is also very likely. However, in nine of the twenty-three cases no agreement was made.

There are also women who opted for another approach. They indicate just what can be possible:
– going on vacation together, a contractual agreement over the ownership of the house if the partner dies, keeping one's own autonomy.

You can make a cohabitation contract with a notary. You can name each other as heir. No one but the notary need know this.

'My friend opted for me. If there were ever problems and he was faced with a choice by the bishop, then he would resign his priestly office. I didn't force him to do this. It was his initiative to make this affidavit with the notary. Emotionally I found that an important event. I really felt that it was a kind of marriage promise, a kind of yes.'

'I usually say that I'm C's friend. I refuse to be swept aside. C loves me, so I'm valuable.'

Although most women indicate that only some people know of their relationship, ten times the relationship is indicated as a 'secret' when questions are asked about the form of the relationship. 'Living apart together' and friendship are mentioned nine times. Once a sexual relationship is mentioned. And once 'incest'.

After the end of my investigation I got another reaction to experiences of incest.

'From my tenth birthday I've been regularly abused sexually. He was a friend of the family and nineteen years older than me. He talked me into a convent. Then he stopped. I know that for a long time there was a photograph of me in nun's clothes on his desk. Now there's a photo of another girl, a child of around eleven.'

What do women feel about their relationship?

There were several possible answers to this question. 'Happy' was said thirteen times; ten times the relationship was described as 'frustrating'; 'painful' was mentioned eight times and also 'satisfying' and 'very happy'. 'Helping each other' was mentioned seven times.

How do women think that the partner feels about the relationship?

Priests are supposed to be happier than their women and their relationship more satisfying. They are thought to find the relationship less 'painful' than the women. Against eight instance of 'painful' for women, there are only five for men. In 'helping the other' the figures are: women seven times, men twice.

There is also a difference between the priests and their women over finding the relationship 'frustrating': women ten times and men four times.

A priest writes about the experience of the relationship:

'The so-called third way is humiliating for the woman and makes her and really also the man a split personality, whereas human beings are created in God's image and likeness.'

A woman who had a relationship for four years writes:

'Really it was doomed to failure from the start. We both had guilt feelings. I had a strict Catholic upbringing and when something terrible happened I thought that it was God's punishment.'

Another woman wrote:

'I was a priest's woman for a while and it almost finished me off.'

The publicity over the often less successful relationships

produced a number of anonymous letters. Someone who knew such a situation from her own experience reacted negatively.

'I don't see how you dare go into this area. Who are you to support women who live in mortal sin?'

There are also women who report that they are happy. However, they often indicate that they had to work hard for that happiness. It didn't come automatically. Their own job and their own identity had a positive influence here.

'I think that in fact we could maintain a good relationship because we both wanted an independent life. I feel that my relationship is positive, but that doesn't meant that it doesn't have its painful aspect. It didn't come automatically. In my case, no children of my own.'

'But I'm happy. With him I find all I ever dreamed of in a man.'

Every relationship has positive and negative sides. In general people invest in a relationship because it is ultimately profitable for them, because the number of positive aspects is greater than that of the negative ones. But not everyone 'weighs' in the same way. I asked the respondents to name positive and negative things.
Positive things mentioned were:
– warmth and tenderness
– shared interest in work
– the things that people look for in a partner generally
– a partner with an understanding and helping character.
The fact of the partner being a priest also played a part: it can be exciting, but it can also make you reflect on church structures.

'But I continue to remember, especially from the initial period, that it was something special to be chosen by a priest. I went to communion with head held high. I never felt bad in this relationship, though people wanted to give me that feeling. I felt above their gaze.'

'It never disturbed me so much that I didn't come first. You knew that if you had a relationship with a priest.

Among the negative aspects, his priesthood and the consequences were mentioned often: the secrecy, his absence, his training, his sexual behaviour. Another negative factor felt was that the partner was sometimes sharing a bed with other women at the same time. Of the twenty-three respondents nine found this, and two didn't know.

'I was so often excluded and could never meet him freely in his own surroundings.'
'I always had to fit in with his situation and be on my guard, so I was always uncertain about the next meeting. Always had to understand his situation. We couldn't be together in public, which meant not showing who you were. In the long run it was humiliating and hurtful. In my view it caused an unnecessary amount of suffering, also for him. When he lived alone I could only come when it suited him. So in fact he determined how often we met. Because he had a relationship with another woman, who needed his help, I always had to be "strong" for him, always had to understand.'
'I had to adapt myself to him in everything and just wait.'
'The relationship took a great deal of energy. You couldn't be yourself with your partner in company. You always had to keep your thoughts and feelings in check. You couldn't be open to others, because you had to keep quiet about some of your inner feelings. It's difficult to trust another person on an unequal basis.'

One woman expresses very clearly what the training of a priest means for her relationship:

'The intense training of the priest, which makes it difficult for him to enter into intimate personal relationships, makes me feel that it is more difficult to talk about the relationship itself than about a relationship with a non-priest.'

Mutual characteristics

Perhaps some priests are attractive to women because they have a number of characteristics which are particularly valued by women.

I asked what characteristics these were. The result was a picture of the man with more gentle characteristics: listening, understanding, being concerned with people, emotional and caring, and with cultural and musical interests.

'His patience, the attention and care with which he does things. Tenderness, love, conversations.'
'He was very sensitive, very musical.'
'Humour, like an a jolly ostrich, and that was sometimes comic. Understanding, listening, a sense of justice, a capacity to persevere, steadfastness.'

I also asked what properties it ws thought that the priest valued most in a woman. The same properties were mentioned, and along with them spontaneity, openness, gaiety and feminist thought. This agreed with what I heard when I met with a number of women.

'My spontaneity and ability to make contacts easily.'
'What he called my authenticity.'
'My tenderness, femininity, homeliness, erotic sexuality, my "help".'
'Openness, honesty, youth, sympathy, qualities as a supervisor, care.'
'My spontaneity, creativity. My attention and concern for his feelings. That I saw him as a person and not as a priest. The atmosphere that I can make and radiate.'
'Openness, independence, capacity to make contact, drive.'

Priests sometimes have a relationship with a woman with children. In my investigation this was the case in seven instances: in two the relationship with the children was felt to be positive:

'After a few meetings, one evening he came along to meet the children, about whom he had heard so much. My oldest son was then seventeen. Things clicked with them immediately. We've always been open towards the children; we've expressed our love. Their reaction was: "Splendid, mother, in that case you must live together." '

A woman whose relationship had been broken off writes:

'A small child was also involved, who from one day to the next lost his "father"; this was an amputation of feelings, a trauma for which the priest doesn't want to bear any responsibility.'

Sex

The questionnaire asked about the women's sexual experience. Of the twenty-three women who answered, twenty-two had a relationship which was also sexual. One woman replied that a clear agreement was made for a non-sexual relationship.

Thirteen of the twenty-two women were positive about sex. Eight were negative, and one said that after a process of adjustment the experience became satisfying.

'For me it meant that now I was the one with experience, whereas in other relationships the men usually thought that they knew everything... Our sex life was no less than in other relationships, just different. Above all the last time I felt that he was more daring than before. For me the church's prohibition has never for a moment been an obstacle to going to bed with him.'

'I'm very happy with our sex life. For me it's good, inspiring, safe, warm, respectful. Being considerate about me, about each other.'

'At times we've petted a lot, indeed brought each other to a climax, but at his request no intercourse.'

'I didn't like it, found it ugly, and now and then he was very rough. Then I usually went "out of my body", I really loathed his body.' This woman was forced into a sexual relationship at a young age. The priest was a friend of the family and she called her relationship incestuous.

'To me it meant nothing because I already knew that afterwards he would regret the "mistake". He couldn't do without it; often I gave in just to please him.'

The women were also asked what they thought the sexual experience of their partner was. Above all, to begin with it was a new experience for their partners, which on the one hand was exciting and enriching and on the other often went with guilt feelings and a sense of having transgressed against church norms.

There is a recurrent dilemma here. Confrontation with one's sexuality in later life often also seems to provoke questions about one's potency and the possibility of satisfaction.

'As a small revelation that sexuality and emotion have become very important in his life.'
'To begin with it was above all anxious and frustrating for him, and the day after he had pangs of conscience over his celibacy.'
'He couldn't control himself, but felt guilty.'
'He was proud of his potency; that gave him a kick.'
'Physical proximity makes him feel human.'

From a letter:

'To begin with, intercourse was threatening for him. He thought it splendid to pet and to be caressed, particularly the latter. It was a surprise to find that there was someone who loved him. And I was good at that. Really he learned a lot from me. Later he was also proud of this. With patience and practice our relationship became very satisfying in the sexual sphere. We made love a lot. Up to the moment when I noticed that he was putting what he had learned into practice with other women. Did it sometimes give him a kick to be such a good lover? There happened to be women who themselves had had an unhappy relationship and sought consolation with him. He found it quite normal to do this. If other women needed him, he had to give himself to them. He couldn't be exclusively for one person; he had to be there "for all".'

I've already mentioned how many women found it a negative

factor that their partner was maintaining several sexual relationships at the same time. This was the case with nine women out of the group of twenty-two. It emerges that at the request of the priest no intercourse then took place.

Of the twenty-three respondents ten women wrote that they were the 'first woman' of their partner. Three women didn't know. In five cases contact with the priest was the 'first man' in their lives. In nine of the twenty-three cases there was equality; both had had an earlier experience, or both had their first experience with each other.

The influence of the relationship

Any relationship has a particular influence on your life. What influence has the relationship (had) on the lives of these women?

Of the twenty-three women, four give a negative answer, naming the church structures as negative factors. One women calls it the 'institute for misogyny'. Three women give a qualified reaction. The others give an answer which can be applied to any good relationship, to which the priesthood of the partner often gives a special colouring.

'My spiritual experience has also become greater. I've begun to steep myself in religion.'
'Priests are also just ordinary people who are not made of stone.'
'It's determined my inner growth and my maturing.'
'In the end I began to study and think in feminist terms, as a result of him.'

Among priests it emerges that the discovery of feelings and sexuality are important. This can give both a positive and a threatening feeling.

'Anxiety about sex overcome.'
'He couldn't or daren't give himself completely at that time, couldn't really enjoy it; of course he did, but afterwards it was always for me: he did it for me and as a reward he also found it good.'

'He's learned to understand women better.'
'An enrichment to his pastoral work and in his own world of feelings.'
'Thanks to our relationship he's come to see that his choice of the priesthood twenty-five years ago wasn't based on a call but on an inability and anxiety over sharing and living with a woman. Celibacy was then a way out.'
'A development from half a person to a whole person (his own words).'

To the question what influence the relationship has had on the women's lives the answer was that for both the relationship has a very uncertain future and that 'a high price has to be paid for it', as a woman put it in a letter.

I found this question very important, because here there can be an expression of where a relationship with a priest differs from that with an 'ordinary' man. It appears that a greater awareness can develop, with both women and men. And also such a relationship can open people's eyes to the difficulty, if not impossibility, of it. This also applies both to women and to men. Their relationship forces the women and the priests to think about their life, their ministry, the situation. Sometimes this leads the men to break off the relationship, sometimes to a deepening of it. After the investigation I got a lot of letters. There were a number of women who had once had a secret relationship with a priest and after breaking it off couldn't tell anyone about it. They sat there with unassimilated sorrow which affected their lives.

'It's now sixteen years ago. I don't know whether he's still alive. Sometimes I want to see him and talk about it.'
'During our relationship and afterwards I often felt desperate because I couldn't talk about it. I needed a woman to whom I could express my personal feelings. I still feel pain, sorrow, the secret.'
'Now I must try again to break through my loneliness. Seek contact with people of my own age. But this experience has made me older, harder.'
'First of all I learned how important it is to care for each other. I think that all this has made me much gentler, certainly to

others in every respect. But above all I've become aware of what a need there is in the sexual sphere.'
'I'd love to talk about it, since I can't get away from it.'

There seem to be women who for a long time couldn't talk about it and now see a possibility which they grasp eagerly.

'Clearly I still need to get my own story of my chest, although it happened a long time ago, around ten years.'

After a relationship which lasted sixteen years but is now broken off, a woman writes:

'Working through such a break is a process of mourning. It isn't easy and I have the feeling that I have to work through it, in secret, alone.'
'All in all it lasted twenty-four years. That was an important part of my life in which in the first instance I had the opportunity to become independent in and through the work that we did together. In this period I helped him through the greatest crisis of his life, a crisis which we endured and lived through together. I showed solidarity in that, sometimes against my better judgment, because I thought that he needed support.'
   Factors which also have a great influence are:
– obligatory celibacy and its consequences
– the need to keep a relationship and sexual feelings secret and unexpressed.
   This applies to the priests, but both factors have consequences for the women.
   This pressure makes some women aware of the consequences of their love; later, others feel used.
'It's made me seek deeper levels in myself and is still the motive force which pushes me towards deeper levels in my awareness of what a relationship is, who I am in my male and female sides and where my illusions are.'
'Through the uncertainty which his priesthood and the lack of clarity in our relationship produce, the feeling creeps up on me that it could suddenly be over. Not that our relationship is

about to fall apart, but if he should die now, almost no one would know that we belong together.'

'The influence was very great, isolated me a lot and stood in the way of my own development.'

At what phase of their lives were the women when the relationship came into being?

Many are mentioned: the phase of discovery, growing phase, stable phase, but also a problem phase, a period of mourning after death or divorce. It can be said that ten women were in a more or less unstable period as the result of a negative experience in their lives.

One woman says, 'I felt fine, so it was not born out of need.' Another says that she was in a stable phase.

Also mentioned is a phase of great respect for the Roman Catholic church.

The church

All the questions in the questionnaire were put to women. Where they related to the priest the woman said what she thought her partner felt. The aim was to discover what the woman feels/felt about the relationship, and so women were asked how they thought their partner stood towards the church, which officially forbids their relationship. Five times the answer was that he had problems with it. In two instance it was not discussed, and five relationships were carried on as if the woman were an ordinary acquaintance, of course to avoid problems with the church:

'A super-denier; he has many problems with himself and the church.'

It is also important to know that ten times it was said that the partner had no problems with the church.

Of the twenty-three respondents, one indicated that her partner no longer had any contact with the church.

Of the twenty-two practising priests who at the same time have (or have had) a relationship with a woman, ten say that they have no problems with the church.

To the question whether the partner feels opposition to the church the answer is 'yes' six times, 'no' three times, 'don't know' three times, 'sometimes' once; once the question is thought too complicated and once the partner is said already to have grown out of the church. The purpose of this question was not to investigate the degree of loyalty to the church among priests who have a relationship with a woman. However, the attitude of the man to the church certainly plays a role in the relationship with his woman. I shall come back to that later.

In ten women with a relationship which had been broken off, only once is opposition to the church to be discovered with the partner. Five times there is 'no opposition', three times the answer is 'don't know' and once 'sometimes'.

What about the women themselves? Do women who repeatedly feel that they are second-class beings who are having a forbidden relationship with a priest which can have consequences for their work, their social relationships, also feel opposed to the church?

Of the twelve women who have a relationship, seven say 'yes', two say 'no' and two 'sometimes'.

With the group which has a relationship that has been broken off, ten in all, I arrive at the following figures: seven say 'yes', two 'no', one finds opposition too strong a term since she herself works in the church. The woman with the latent relationship which has still to be ended says 'yes'.

Of the twenty-three women, fifteen give an unqualified yes as an answer.

'Only when I was no longer needed did a crisis occur for me, in the first instance with sorrow and pain, and later with anger and disappointment. But that has made me mature and only as a result have I grown up. Fortunally no rancour remains.'
'I began to see him and the whole situation of the church, the order and priesthood more sharply and began to see it more as it really was. To begin with, I projected my ideal pictures of the male and the priest on to him and consequently remained blind to his mistakes and shortcomings. At a later stage I did see them, but didn't accept them because I couldn't believe that he was like that.

Now it's as it is, he's as he is and I'm as I am, and no
relationship between us fits into that.'

Women whose relationship had been broken off were asked
whether they would want to enter into a relationship with a priest
again. Six women answered 'no' and three said 'perhaps, but not
a secret one again'.

'Really the question "Is God a woman?" is the wrong one. The
right question which women and thoughtful people put at present
is: "Is God a man?" Do you think, dear priests and scribes,
ministers and professors, all men for two thousand years, that
you can tell us that God is a man? And conclude from this that
men are higher, better, more intelligent and stronger?

God must definitely be more than a man, otherwise God isn't
God. God is also more than a woman. God has created male and
female, so they must both be in God, the male and the female.
They must be strong and able to love; I say that because I can call
God both "he" and "she". I can pray "Our father and mother
who art in heaven..." If I only think "he", then my God is a bit
too small. Perhaps too churchy, perhaps also too worldly, namely
psychologically no more developed than many men I know.
Because I don't want too small a God, sometimes I call God she.
She protects you. She helps you, she is just and good.'

(from Dorothee Sölle, 'Und es ist noch nicht erschienen, was wir
sein werden.' Stationen feministischer Theologie)

Conclusions

The previous chapter gave a brief summary account of the results of the questionnaire from twenty-three women. The answers given by the women seem very different. But common features can be discovered. These also emerged at the meetings which were held later.

Now an answer can be given to the questions:
– What do women feel about a relationship with a priest?
– Are there specific problems in it?
– What can be done about these problems?

Certain conclusions can be drawn. It is important for women to know whether they can do anything about the problems in their relationship, though some cannot be solved. Obligatory celibacy will not be abolished immediately. But is there a margin within which you can change things so that the problems can be reduced? To find an answer to that it is necessary first to answer the questions above.

The experience of the relationship

First the social experience, the outside. Women experience a relationship with a priest as an extremely secret or more or less secret relationship which officially has no right to exist. Certainly not within the church, which threatens all kinds of reprisals like expulsion, transfer or dismissal. This has consequences, both material and non-material, for the situation of the priest's partner. If he finds himself on the street without a job, and with no income, that can also have consequences for his woman. He can be stripped of the status which his ministry has always given him. Women share with their partners this tension caused by the threat of social and psychological breakdown. Some priests are in places where they can carry on their relationship relatively undisturbed, but there are also priests who have a child in the utmost secrecy. Doubtless this puts heavy pressure on the woman and on the education of the child.

Living together, sleeping together, having vacations together, going out, shopping, walking arm in arm, visiting families is rarely if ever possible. There is really no possible way of fulfilling the wish to have children.

There are many answers to the question what women feel about the relationship in their social life. But two groups must be distinguished. The first group keep the relationship extremely secret and there is no social life at all. The second group of women have given their relationship a social significance to a greater or lesser degree. Sometimes this relationship is known within a small circle, and attempts are made to extend this circle, or the woman quite openly joins in and says precisely what the position is.

The first group have such limited relations with the outside world that communication with this outside world as a couple is impossible. When there are problems, this outside world cannot function as a source of help. The limitation of this group is too tight, and very negative for the success of the relationship, because problems have to be solved within the relationship itself. This can cause many tensions.

For the success of the relationship it is generally better if the outside world knows. If women of priests also want to give their relationship a certain openness, then they come up against the other dilemma: church sanctions. Perhaps for the moment it is best to take a middle course. That means making the relationship known to parents, friends and acquaintances. This makes healthy social contact and control possible. It establishes the identity of the couple, because people get to know them as they are, as people who have chosen each other.

It is also loyal to each other. Women should require their relationship to be known to at least a number of people. For women in particular this part of their emotional life is very important, to know and make it be known that 'I belong to him, even if he is a priest.' It is no coincidence that it is important for the identity of women to indicate who their partner is. That is the way in which women were once brought up.

Social recognition brings us closer within. Experience of identity is a feeling which is experienced both in social and in personal being. The sociologist Lillian B.Rubin describes how women and men balance their experience of love and work in different ways. For women, being a wife and mother is an essential part of their identity and of essential importance for their own worth. For men the important part lies in the work that they do. The origin of this difference lies, Lillian Rubin says, in the difference between rational and cognitive characteristics. Work is mastery, achievement; love has to do with giving meaning. Love and work move men and women in different ways. Men have relatively stronger ego boundaries than women. So they also experience things differently. Both men and women have their socialization from baby girl to woman and baby boy to man to thank (or to blame) for this. Whereas the man is more orientated on his status outside the home, the woman finds the inner world more important. For women emotions weigh heavier; women attach value to a continuity in relations with another person. As a result the separation of the private and the public identity of the secret relationship will probably be harder for the woman than for the man. For the man, the priest, the greatest satisfaction is in his office, the priesthood, and training for that determines his identity to a great degree. Precisely because he is a man, he has less difficulty in keeping his work and his private life separate.

Women do not have a positive view of the image of the institution to which he is bound; many women feel this way. We often hear how and what a woman needs to be. The fact that she is a woman imposes a great many limitations. Although the partner of the priest wants to show that she has her own identity (that she is neither 'madonna' nor 'slut'), she may not, because the institution to which her man is bound and to which he must be loyal prohibits a relationship with her.

The woman of a priest cannot therefore show herself as she really is: she is prevented from becoming visible by her partner.

For years the woman's movement has striven to make visible the place of women within society: work at home, caring for the household, giving love and attention, the functions of cherishing and welcoming.

It emerges from the investigation that there are women who

have taken this step. They have clearly demonstrated that they are the woman of a priest. They tell the bishop, they write to the superior, a letter which they sign 'the woman of Fr X', and talk about their situation at work. These are all signs of opposition to the oppressive situation in which they find themselves.

How do women feel about the fact that the hierarchy maintains that celibacy is a permanent vow while knowing full well that relationships exist? No recognition of a priest's partner is possible, but obviously partners are tolerated. Is this a marginal existence? What other factors make the relationship so valuable if this is 'swallowed'?

Women have all kinds of feelings about their relationship. For them the experience is less 'happy 'and more 'frustrating' than for their priests.

Other negative aspects in addition to secrecy which are mentioned are: his frequent absence, his sexual behaviour, being able to talk a lot about others but not about yourself, hiding behind his office, not being there when you need him.

And yet, on average, relationships last around ten years and those that are broken off around nine. Why do women keep up such a 'frustrating' relationship for so long? Does this lie in the nature of women?

A woman who had a very long relationship with a priest wrote that in the end he married another woman. She literally wrote, 'as long as he's happy'. I ask myself why this woman never asked anything for herself.

'To love someone is perhaps the most difficult of all tasks for a human being, the extreme, the last test, the work for which everything else is mere preparation' (Rainer Maria Rilke).

'In the holistic experience of love, feeling, knowing and understanding can go together... This is love in which people feel bound to a greater whole' (I. Weeda).

Why do women fall in love with a priest? What has attracted them? Many of the positive characteristics mentioned here also exist in an 'ordinary' relationship, though some do not. It is striking that trust and tenderness are mentioned more than once.

There are views about intimacy in a relationship which claim that women want intimacy and that men are opposed to it. There is another view which says that men indeed seek intimacy, but express it in a different way. This comes about as a result of their childhood years, in which they have systematically learned to put their feelings in the background. By contrast, women are encouraged to develop their feelings, emotions and fantasies.

Women also convey faith to their children. They have also learned from their religion to be of service (despite the story of Martha and Mary). In earlier forms of marriage service (up to around 1945) the woman was asked to obey her husband, serve him and help him. Society expects women to be submissive and obedient (happily this is changing) and the church sanctions this in the spiritual sphere.

Women support their priests, and it is very possible that they put this serving, or allow it to be put, in the perspective of the church. Women are also more affected by church life: on Sunday there are more women than men in church, they hand down the faith, they fulfil diaconal functions, they look after the flowers and visit the sick, but the men rule the church.

I don't want to suggest that a woman who has a relationship with a priest by definition serves the church with her faith and therefore accepts everything from her partner. But I do ask myself whether the experience of belief weakens the making of demands in the relationship. Is opposing your man more or less the same thing as opposing the rules of God which have put man above women? The priest as a 'man with an exclusive calling' again occupies a special place here.

There is no indication why a relatively large number of respondents began their relationship after 1980. There could be more than one reason: the greater openness about relations in society, despondency over the expected abolition of celibacy, or the fact that the partners were 'in the prime of middle age' (between forty and sixty), a time when one weighs up one's life and explores new situations.

'*Above all there is a search for intensification, for developing the inner life. Jung already observed forcefully that what has not developed continues to press for unfolding. Age-old archaic forms of experience claim their due, the lost relationship with the collective unconscious, the archetypes and primal types of human existence are activated anew. Everything breaks loose, and repressed tenderness rises to the surface. In those who are bound up in themselves and not in a position to surrender, sometimes a desire to let rip emerges'* (H.C.Rümke, *Levenstijdperken van de man*).

A number of women teach their partner how to fit sex into his life as an enriching experience. Often women meet a partner who has learned to see sex as a negative element in his life. A number of women succeed in building up a satisfactory sexual relationship, perhaps because they know that the man must undergo the same sort of process of emancipation as they did to begin with.

Behind closed doors women help clergy over their relational and sexual barriers and here, without intending it, are serving the church. For the priest who experiences this process of liberation will radiate it in his preaching and his pastoral work.

'It is not that, as traditional views have it, the sexual reactions of a woman are more moderate than those of a man or that she has no need or desire for sexual release. Since a girl, if she later wants to be in a position to form a sexual bond with a man, must as a child repress the erotic aspect of her earliest tie, the explicitly sexual element occupies a less autonomous place in her inner life. A man can desire women, but a woman desires a man. For women, sexuality generally has significance only in the context of a relationship – which may explain why so many girls as adolescents or young adults seldom if ever masturbate' (Lillian B.Rubin, *Intimate Strangers*)

Rubin describes how the emotional bond in women is usually a stimulus to, if not a condition of, eroticism. Among women, the sexual is aroused by the emotional bond. In men it is the other way round: they hope that an emotional bond will come about through the sexual bond. This is because entering into an emotional tie is so difficult for men, as a result of the impossibility for the male infant to identify with his mother, his earliest emotional tie. He suppresses it, but the erotic aspect remains, later to be directed to other women.

Permanently having to be available 'for the church', as men put it, is sometimes used as an excuse for several sexual relationships at the same time. During their training priests are taught to be always there for all people and not to have any exclusive relations with particular individuals. There are women who accept that their partner will have several loves. This can be a norm a person has clearly chosen. It can be that women have taken over to such a degree the norms and values that priests themselves apply about having to be available for others that they agree with them that in their situation it is 'right' to maintain several relationships at the same time. Precisely because they believe that they have to be available for all.

Having several sexual relationships at the same time can be an indication of anxiety about too great an emotional invovlement. We also know that emotional involvement is often a condition for women being able to enter into a satisfying sexual relationship. Why does a women whose partner has several relationships keep hers going? Can it be that for too long she has been accustomed to others, men, taking the decisions?

Women often feel resistance to the church. That is understandable, since you have to be doubly subordinate: in your position as a woman and as the partner of a priest. If you are a believer you must keep your belief and the church well apart in your experience, otherwise you run the risk of losing your faith... If the partner himself is also opposed to the church, you can share this resistance. But in that case something else may happen; he leaves the church and has to find a career.

Women with a relationship which has been broken off continue to maintain the resistance they have shown during their relationship. Often they can't talk about their disillusionment. If your partner leaves you in the lurch after years of living together, there is no obligation to alimony. You cannot claim any support from the father of your child except by legal proceedings.

'Life can only be understood in retrospect, but it has to be lived forward.'

*'To use someone to find satisfaction or security is not love.
Love is no security; love is a state in which the longing for
security does not exist; it is a vulnerable condition'*

(J.Krishnamurti).

Why do women opt for such a relationship?

'I think that's a stupid question. I'm in love with him and he's in
love with me.'

That's a very concrete answer, but there are other reasons why
women can feel attracted to a priest. The psychiatrist Jürg Willi
has written at length about this choice of partner. In the choice of
a partner there is a certain agreement in terms of class, race,
religion, view of life, norms and values, attitude, habits and
interests. Willi argues that in an encounter people begin to 'colour'
themselves in accordance with the expectation of the other,
because they feel best in an environment where they are accepted.
He sees the choice of a partner as a two-sided process of adaptation
in which an important part of the needs, anxieties and ideals
becomes extra-important, whereas other facets of the personality
are little affected by the choice of partner. This can also be seen
in the formation of other relationships, at work or among friends.
A collusion can arise from this reciprocal process of adaptation:
by this Willi understands the unrecognized interplay of partners,
which is often unconscious, an interplay that they set up and keep
going by the anxieties and the guilt-feelings which they share
with each other, to defend and to conquer, by which they feel
inescapably bonded to each other.

If we think of women who love too much, as Robin Norwood
describes them, and we look for a partner who would fit this
collusion, then we arrive at a partner who yearns for the affection
of a woman.

This partner wants to be looked after and protected; he seeks
security with her. She presents herself as the great mother,
someone who will make all his dreams come true and will
magically change him into her true prince. But she will be the one
who does it. Perhaps she will make all his dreams come true and

sacrifice herself wholly for him. However, behind all her concern lurks the great anxiety that one day he will no longer need her. Behind his insatiable need for attention and security he hides his anxiety about being disappointed. He is afraid of being rejected.

He is often pampered in his youth and wants a bit of that. And the woman is ready to give him everything. She has learned not to ask anything for herself. She can't do that directly. When she tried earlier she was punished. She can only receive something if she herself gives a great, great deal. And for that she gets her reward. For the time being. For he will become constantly more demanding. And the more she gives, the more gratitude she will require. So people end up in a vicious circle. It is important to know that such circles do not make them happy. These circles have more to do with fulfilling one's own need for attention and security than with love. At the end of such a relationship amazement often surfaces: how can this be, after I've given him all he wanted and he still wasn't satisfied, while I expected so little for myself?

There is a way of getting out of such collusion. In brief, it amounts to accepting yourself. Trying to become aware of your own feelings. Giving yourself reassurance instead of always requiring it from others. If you then come to realize that such a relationship is destructive for you, you have the courage to break it off. You aren't letting demands be made on you, but for once are asking something for yourself.

Having a relationship gives someone a nice sense of belonging. Because by their upbringing women are above all endowed with relational capacities, it is not so surprising that they look for a relationship in which they can also use these properties. As a result of their upbringing men are above all equipped to move in the outside world. So it also understandable that the intimacy which women seek above all in a relationship is difficult to achieve. It emerges from the questionnaire that it is indeed often difficult to achieve true intimacy in relationships with a priest. The conditions for a healthy relationship are marginal. Certainly as a woman you should be well aware of these things. It seems that the partner can find greater satisfaction in the relationship because his emotional needs can easily be fulfilled by many women.

In her book *The Future of Marriage*, Jessie Bernard points out that traditionally marriage is seen by men as a trap: 'Once you're married that's the end of the sweet life.' By contrast, men think that for women marriage is a lottery. In practice, however, the opposite is the case: married men live longer; marriage is a great help in their social life and in their professional career. Psychologically, marriage makes a positive contribution and offers them protection against depressions. It offers them emotional security and a secure status.

Traditionally, all women want to marry. Clearly marriage is attractive. But statistically, married women have more problems with different forms of depression, are more discontented over marriage than men, and mention more problems. In Jessie Bernard's investigation it emerges that marriage is a greater 'gain' for men than for women.

It is an open question whether all this also applies to a relationship without marriage, a relationship which can last for years. Women often find that they experience their relationship with a priest as a marriage. Perhaps that is true of the emotional security which they offer their partner. This is above all what men look for and it gives them more balance in their lives.

And women? What is their 'gain'? If the relationship is an equal one, then it is clear that the women have also learned to ask something for themselves. This means openness, at least making the relationship known to some extent, becoming visible, and not being too bothered about the antiquated norms of the church.

That can mean that you do not accept your partner going along with these old norms. Partners may expect understanding from each other and a real furthering of their own development. It is a fluctuating pattern of supporting and being supported, being open and honest to each other. To grow in that direction, in secret, against the commandments and judgments of the church and the prevailing 'picture of women', is definitely not easy, and may certainly be called a task.

'*Let me tell you my fantasy about the "man with a heart": for me he is the positive inward male figure who emerges from a healthy relationship with one's father. First he is caring, warm and strong. He is not afraid of anger, nor of intimacy and love. He sees through the bewitching, the artificial defence-mechanisms of the essential in me. He stays with me and is patient. But he takes initiatives, he confronts me and is also himself on the move. He is stable and patient. But his stability comes from the fact that he joins in the streams of life, that he lives in the here and now. He plays and works and enjoys both, he feels at home wherever he is – in the inner world or the outside world. He is a man of the earth, instinctive and sexual, and he is a man of the spirit, exalted and creative. He loves nature, animals, birds, flowers, woods, mountains, meadows, rivers and the sea. He loves children and the inner child. He loves the change of the seasons. He can enjoy the beginning of spring, relax in the powerful ripening of summer, mature in the colourful late glory of the fall, deepen himself in the stillness of the winter snow; and then be open again to the spring that is born anew. He loves beauty, art, words and music. Perhaps he sings or plays the bassoon or violin and he dances to the rhythm of life. He is the comrade of your soul, your inner friend and love who goes with you, a woman, on the adventurous journey through life.'*

(Linda Leonard, *Wounded Woman*).

Can you do anything about these problems?

What constantly kept emerging in the short meetings and individual conversations as ways of coping with the problems of a relationship with a priest included these points:
– You can make yourself so strong, possibly along with other women, that you have the courage to mske yourself known as his partner. Do this step by step and think of the possible repercussions.
– As 'colleagues' you can get together to exchange experiences, good and bad, and ideas to widen both personal and social actions.
– You can decide that such a relationship asks too much of you and put an end to it.
– Take good care of yourself well, live your own life, be aware of your own basic needs and see that they are sufficiently met. Don't

let everything depend on your partner. Don't let him hide behind his vcocation. Don't take more than half the responsibility for maintaining the relationship with you. Be aware of your own qualities.

– Try to learn the things you find negative. Resentment doesn't help; mistakes are your friends on the way to tomorrow.

– Don't let yourself be forced into a corner by the church, but keep your own faith alive. Try to join in where people are working for renewal.

– Show solidarity with other women and men who are fighting the same battle.

The meetings

1. *The reason*

The result of the investigation shows that there are good reasons for accepting that many women who have a relationship with a priest find this relationship problematical.

There are few people with whom they can talk about it, they can have hardly any exchanges, and their personality threatens to be overshadowed.

I asked the women whether they would like to meet one another. To this nine replied 'yes' and ten 'perhaps, it depends'. Of the women who had an existing relationship (thirteen), six said yes. Of the women whose relationship had been broken off (ten) three said yes. In the end twelve people could meet. First they had all received the results of the questionnaire.

2. *The aim*

The aim of the meetings was:
– an exchange of experiences
– to discover points where they wanted changes to make the relationship happier
– to work through old hurts – to develop ideas for improving the situation
    I had set myself two secondary aims
– to investigate whether the result of the questionnaire was right
– to investigate whether my conclusions fitted.

3. The method

I organized two meetings, one for women with positive experiences and one for women with predominantly negative experiences. I made this distinction because it emerged from the questionnaire that women's experinces were very different and it seemed that they also viewed their relationships in very different ways, from very positive to hostile. It didn't seem to me viable to confront a group with such great differences.

The invitation contained the necessary conditions for the meeting:
– confidentiality and secrecy
– contributing something, learning something that could be done
– a social element, by getting together.

Here is an account of the meetings.

Meeting 1

This meeting was for women who have or have had predominantly positive experiences.

The atmosphere was excellent; the women began talking very soon.

A woman was present at this meeting who had a non-sexual relationship. Although her situation differed from that of the other women, there was the best possible mutual respect.

The answers to the question why the women had reacted to the advertisement were as follows:

'I wanted to get to know women in the same situation.'
'I was curious whether there were other women and I wanted to talk to them about it, something I've never done.'
'It's time that this problem came out into the open. That people begin to understand what is happening.'

That was a good opening for going further with telling their own stories. Here the women were very open. They asked each other now and then to clarify things and gave a positive feedback. While they were telling their life stories it proved that some women had stood up for themselves well in the relationship: they had put it all on paper. This was very valuable for the others present. The relationship of two women had been broken off, that of the others had not. Later it proved that the women had actually used suggestions that had been made.

What are the strong points within the relationship?
This is an important condition for change. You can exploit your strong points.
  The following emerged:

> patience – balance – humour – the ability to relativize – the ability to share thought – the capacity for empathy – being able to create companionship – being strong – being able to listen – making it possible to discuss experiences and feelings – questions about experiences/feelings – spontaneity – openness – being 'in the world'.

What can women themselves change within their relationship?
  'At this moment I don't know.'
  'Don't make such demands on myself and others, including my partner.'
  'Its fine as it is.'
  'I need to indicate my own limits better.'

A number of women thought that things were fine; others wanted to stand up more firmly for themselves.

What is different about a relationship with a priest?
  'In the first place a priest opts for his fellow priests, the work always comes first.'
  'Priest-partners find it more difficult to talk about themselves than other men.'
  'A man who is utterly tied to his office always remains a priest, even if he comes out and no longer works as a pastor.'
  'Such a relationship produces contradictory feelings: on the one hand you invest a lot, and on the other you remain invisible.'
  'There is no natural attitude to the outside world.'

What can you do about the specific problems?

'In order to be able to live together we found two flats next door to each other, but with separate doors.'

'You can't marry, but you can make a contract with a notary. We have a photograph of it; for us it's like wedding photographs.'

'Telling my story has done me good.'

The women felt very positive about being able to talk to one another and asked whether it wouldn't make sense next time also to arrange a shadow meeting for their partners.

'They never talk to one another about it.'

'My partner would like that very much.'

All the women agreed that there must be some publicity about what it's like to be the woman of a priest. This openness has a twofold aim; there is no longer any possibility of denying their existence and it also gives support to other women.

There were some reactions at the end of the meeting.

'I got something from the stories of others, good tips.'

'It's good to look back and see that I've completely changed in my relationship.'

'I felt a bond with the others. I very much valued the openness.'

'A special day, I enjoyed it very much.'

'My relationship is different but no less. I ask myself whether our men won't be shocked when they read the survey.'

A number of women thought that that might well be the case.

Meeting 2

This meeting was meant for women who had had more negative than positive experiences.

The atmosphere was very good. People listened to each other well. The women could express their feelings to each other well.

Now again the question arose *why they had replied to the advertisement* and *why they had come.*

The reactions were identical.

They wanted to talk with other women about their relationship. They wanted to make themselves visible, because they had always had to remain invisible.

'When my relationship was over I never had the chance to express my feelings to him in a conversation, to say how I had felt about the relationship. I can cope with it better like this.'

What did the women feel about their relationship with a priest and what were the specific problems in it?
'A relationship with a priest is not so natural as an ordinary relationship.'

Women said that the sexuality of priests was very frustrating:

'They never get over their own sexual feelings, which for them are loaded with guilt.'

Adrienne told how her priest friend wanted to go to chapel with her to 'do penance'. She now describes this situation as comical. They had been petting, but no intercourse took place. In his last (farewell) letter, which came unannounced, he wrote about his penitential journey. He presented the pastoral solution: recommended another priest if she still needed someone to talk to. He himself 'opted for Him'. As a priest he regretted that he had not been able to bring her closer to God. He didn't talk about her feelings, which he himself had hurt, but hid behind his vocation.

It also seemed to other women that priests ran away when they were confronted with the feelings of their woman. This was not the same experience as with ordinary people, because priests used their office as an excuse. The 'higher thing, being called to an office'. This belief, often shared with women, was used to camouflage their own inability and shortcomings. 'And that is to lose your faith,' a woman said.

'After my relationship with Bernard I have also lost my feeling of belonging to the church. Now I find the whole church a mass of hypocrisy.'

Petra remarked:

'When by chance I discovered that he was having sexual contact with several women, he justified it like this: priests may never be exclusively for one woman; if other women need a priest, he must "mean" just as much for them (go to bed with them). Earlier he had often told me that I was the only one with whom he had such an intimate relationship.'

Because the relationship must always remain more or less secret, it is not under social control, so that some priests play around rather. Women have also found that when priests run away from a relationship, they take no account of the feeling of their women. It's up and away, with Africa as the favourite place to go to.

As a result of their education, in which the woman is depicted as second-class, it is probable that a number of priests will have even more difficulty than ordinary men with a relationship on an equal footing. There is much more at risk for them if they opt for a relationship with a woman than there is for an ordinary man: loss of face, loss of office, expulsion from the order, being seen as an ordinary man without the exclusive status of the chosen priesthood. One woman thought it quite special at the beginning of her relationship that she had been chosen by a priest.

The experience of the relationship is different for Catholic women and for Protestant women. Non-Catholic women are not put off by the aura of the priest. For them the priest is more an ordinary man with a 'burdensome' profession.

When the relationship is broken there seem to be priests who 'feel trapped by their penis just like other men', as Paula says. After the relationship was broken off her ex-friend wanted to put her out of the house; although she was sick, her priest friend though she was fit to be moved out of the house.

The denial of the intensity of the relationship is expressed regularly.

'You're his niece, his sister or his housekeeper, or you're made completely invisible. The priesthood gives these "incontinent priests" such protection that an outside glance first assumes that there is no relationship or that the father has an attractive niece, or a friend – surely these days priests can at least have a female friend.'

'People see what they want to see.'

Looking back on the meetings

The aim of the meetings was achieved:

– Women were able to exchange feelings and as a result actually do something.

– Women made discoveries. What you could change to make your relationship happier. Here they immediately went into action. Points of 'social action' were prepared.

– Old hurts could be worked through by talking about the relationship in a good atmosphere. It was above all a matter of putting the problems in perspective, without accusing yourself or your partner. A rational approach to the relationship: 'That was the situation then, but now I see it better and I can handle it.'

The women were very satisfied with the account of the investigation. Reading it had done them good, above all had also encouraged them. That was also a strong motivation to come to the meetings. It was thought that the account of the response to the questionnaire gave a proper picture and was an argument for total openness.

Plans for the future

Women who took part in this investigation had no objection to making the findings more widely known. They saw this as a step towards giving themselves a profile as the woman of a priest. It was resolved to offer this investigation to the bishops. All bishops were offered a personal presentation of the results of the enquiry. Four bishops sent an answer. Friendly letters, but personal presentations were not allowed. The results could be sent by post, and this was done. Interest was expressed, and sometimes we were told that after reading the survey the bishop would decide whether an interview was necessary. Nothing was heard from any of the other bishops.

This was a great disappointment for the women.

Network

Meanwhile a network has come into being. Women who want to talk with another woman about their relationship with a priest can make contact by writing to:

Netwerk Philothea
  Postbus 30180
  8003 CD Zwolle, Netherlands

The Philothea network has now received a subsidy for its activity. That means both recognition and the possibility of remaining active.

In conclusion

So far, after a first attempt to deny their existence, from the official side there have so far only been vague descriptions of the women of priests. It is now clear that they do exist. They are often very strong women who support their partner in his work and his struggle within the church.

Many women are emancipated women and perhaps precisely for this reason are attractive as partners to priests who find themselves in a process of renewing their thinking about the church and women.

The partners of these women, the priests, are often men who have gone through the process of achieving awareness with pain and difficulty. As a result they have become more balanced. Often they no longer feel completely at home in the church, but find enough satisfaction, above all in contact with people, for example in base communities, to remain in office.

A group of women try to share their lives with partners who are not emotionally up to it. For this group the relationship is completely secret to the outside world. These are women who find little satisfaction and are unhappy about that. But they do not have the courage to ask more for themselves. If they do try, the priest hides behind his 'special calling' or the relationship goes wrong. If these women finally have the courage to break off the relationship, then they are left with their sorrow and cannot talk about it to anyone.

That is a burden to have to go on carrying around, while they are also robbed of the possibility of learning from a relationship which ultimately went wrong.

The priests who have a secret relationship sometimes do not

hesitate to abuse their partner. Their official life and their life in that relationship are in stark contrast. But this life remains secret because they are able to convince their partner that it must remain so. And so everything remains covered with the 'mantle of love'. The woman swallows this, also because as a woman she has learned to adapt to the man. They maintain a relationship which really frustrates them. Faith and the rule that applies within it, that the man, and certainly the priest, stands above the woman, can paralyse the woman who is brought up in this faith, without her wanting or being able to appeal to her own potential to change something in the relationship in her favour. Here is some advice for them:

'Start from the fact that he's an ordinary man, not a saint. Usually he will have little experience of relationships. He will have been brought up differently from you and from other men. Possibly he has a lot to learn and will have to catch up on a delayed puberty.'

There are priests who also themselves suffer as a result of their secret relationship. They suffer as a result of the ban on it and the secrecy which arises around the relationship. Many of these priests feel lonely and are disillusioned with their work, the church and the order. They are trapped in rules which fail to do them justice as human beings. They find compensation in a relationship. For the first time in their lives they encounter human warmth. Their woman friend is often prepared to give it them to a high degree. But the price that she pays for this is high. It is important to say once again that it is not primarily a sexual relationship. That only comes much later.

In the first instance, through contact with one another people expect to be less lonely, to let warmth stream to each other and to feed each other with energy and the joy of life. Initially that seems to succeed. Later the limitations begin to weigh heavy and they grow out of the relationship, or the partners are caught up in a game of anxiety and guilt feelings, which can then be a reason for remaining together without being happy. That is sad, above all if they are afraid of calling in professional help. The threshold which is there for many people seems even higher for relationships with priests.

However, it makes sense to get an insight into one's own conscious and unconscious actions through therapy. For women there is the possibility of making contact with the Philothea network. At different places in the Netherlands women are ready to talk with other women: 'to be a listening soul and a helping hand.'

This book has discussed relationships between women and priests. It is well known that there are also priests who have a homosexual relationship. The partners of these priests largely suffer the same problems as the women in this book. In one particular respect it is even more difficult for them. They are bowed down under an even greater rejection by the institutional church. Because of the difference in upbringing between boys and girls, it seems a possible assumption that men are less prepared than women to allow themselves to be persuaded to keep their relationship secret, because of the 'special situation' of the priest partner. However, to go further would take us outside the framework of this investigation.

Men as a group keep the institutional church in being and women their secret relationship. Women should be able to realize that as a group they also have the power to break the tabu round their relationship in being. But the majority of women allow power to be exercised over them: the power of the denial of their relationship with the man they love and whom they support. An important part of their life is thus denied. One of the signs of the power that the church has is that it keeps these relationships quiet. After the first publicity there is a suspicious silence. That is a proven method, keeping quiet so that nothing seems to be going on.

One concern of this book is to oppose the silence. In the first place it is intended for all 'Philotheas' (which in Greek means 'friends of God'), a pseudonym for all women whose social characteristic is that their loved one is a priest, in the hope that they can 'have some prospects', that they can get a better insight into their situation and be in a better position to maintain and make known their identity. You can certainly influence the situation with which you are discontented; you can fight for those things which you find important. Women experience their own power in this dispute. Taking small steps is progress. Many hope to see the abolition of obligatory celibacy, but as long as that point has not been reached, we need to look for small steps we actually can take. One of the starting points of the feminist perspective is that women can best judge for themselves what is good, can take responsibility, can find creative solutions for their problems, and are in a position to do all this to achieve their aims.

'Human beings don't just exist, but always determine what their existence will be, what they will be in the next moment' (Viktor Frankl).

Epilogue

It takes more than one person to produce a book like this. Many people have been involved in it. This book is by all these people. They often entrusted their deepest feelings to me. There were the very first women, the women of the Philothea network: their support was indispensable, and without their practical dedication the network would never have come into being. Contact with them strengthened me in the conviction that if we really wanted to, we could solve many problems. Often that required energy, and sometimes also brought pain. If you can be there for each other at these moments, it is of inestimable worth.

I had the privilege of meeting many inspiring people, people who are trying to live with great awareness. When I try to describe these contacts I find how difficult it is: they were very intense and valuable. But there was also a compensating humour and delight which made these meetings so special. My friend Jannie, who has been looking over my shoulder for more than twenty years, didn't make a specific contribution to this book, but she has done so to my life and thus also to the making of this book.

Had there not been Toos's contribution, this book would have looked very different. And I'm grateful to Leo for all the insights that he provided about his slow growth.

For me the period during which I was writing my dissertation and this book was a good one. It was also a time of much effort and hard work. I was able to share the high points and the low points with my dear ones, Helen, Marco and Inez and with my beloved Pieter. They are part of my life and so they also share in my life. Now and then they felt my struggle to keep the many facets and tasks in my life in balance, as I had chosen.

That's what this book is all about: how to lead your own life within the possibilities and impossibilities that are given.

Some books

Alther, Lisa, *Other Women*, Penguin Books 1986

Bernard, Jessie, *The Future of Marriage*, Bantam Books 1972

Daly, Mary, *Beyond God the Father*, Beacon Press 1973 and The Women's Press 1986

Dowling, Colette, *The Cinderella Complex*, Fontana Books 1982

Ehrenreich, Barbara, *Hearts of Men*, Pluto Publications 1983

French, Marilyn, *Beyond Power*, Cape 1986

Friedan, Betty, *The Feminine Mystique*, Penguin Books 1982

Fromm, Erich, *The Art of Loving*, Allen and Unwin 1957

Gordon, Mary, *Company of Women*, Cape 1981

Harris, Thomas A., *I'm OK, You're OK*, Pan Books 1973

Horney, Karen, *The Neurotic Personality of Our Time*, Routledge 1937

Leonard, Linda, *Wounded Woman*, Swallow Press 1982

Miller, Alice, *The Drama of the Gifted Child*, Faber 1983

Norwood, Robin, *Women who Love Too Much*, Arrow Books 1986

Pohier, Jacques, *God in Fragments*, SCM Press and Crossroad Publishing Company 1986

Rubin, Lillian B., *Women of a Certain Age*, Harper and Row 1981

Sölle, Dorothee, *Und ist noch nicht erschienen, was wir sein werden. Stationen feministischer Theologie*, Deutscher Taschenbuch Verlag, Munich 1987

Waddell, Helen, *Peter Abelard*, Constable 1933

Irving Yalom, *The Theory and Practice of Group Psychotherapy*, Basic Books 1975